THE
LADY
IS A
SPY

THE
LADY
IS A

SPY

VIRGINIA HALL, WORLD WAR II
HERO OF THE FRENCH RESISTANCE

DON MITCHELL

SCHOLASTIC
FOCUS
NEW YORK

All rights reserved. Published by Scholastic Focus, an imprint of Scholastic Inc., *Publishers since 1920.* SCHOLASTIC, SCHOLASTIC FOCUS, and associated logos are trademarks and/or registered trademarks of Scholastic Inc.

Library of Congress Cataloging-in-Publication Data

Names: Mitchell, Don, 1957– author.
Title: The lady is a spy : Virginia Hall, World War II hero of the French resistance / by Don Mitchell.
Description: First edition. | New York, NY : Scholastic Focus, an imprint of Scholastic Inc., 2019. | Audience: Ages 12 and up. | Includes bibliographical references and index.
Identifiers: LCCN 2018037755 | ISBN 9780545936125
Subjects: LCSH: Goillot, Virginia, 1906–1982—Juvenile literature. | Women spies—United States--Biography—Juvenile literature. | Spies—United States—Biography—Juvenile literature. | World War, 1939–1945—Secret service—United States—Juvenile literature. | World War, 1939–1945— Underground movements—France—Juvenile literature. | World War, 1939–1945—Secret service—Great Britain—Juvenile literature. | Espionage, American—Europe—History—20th century—Juvenile literature.
Classification: LCC D810.S8 G59 2019 | DDC 940.54/8673092 [B]—dc23

10 9 8 7 6 5 4 3 2 1   19 20 21 22 23

Printed in the U.S.A. 23

First edition, March 2019

Book design by Kay Petronio

A remarkable woman, of extraordinary courage and formidable tenacity . . . She did not submit easily to discipline, she had the habit of forming her ideas without regard to the views of others, but she rendered inestimable services to the Allied cause and is a very great friend of France.

—Maurice Buckmaster,
head of the SOE's F Section

AUTHOR'S NOTE ON NAMES

During her World War II service, Virginia Hall was known by a number of aliases, or "cover" names, to protect her true identity. This is a common practice in the field of espionage. Her colleagues in British intelligence (the Special Operations Executive, or the SOE), US intelligence (the Office of Strategic Services, or the OSS), and the French Resistance would know her by a variety of names, including: Diane, Marie Monin, Philomène, Brigitte Le Contre, Renée, Marcelle Montagne, Nicolas, Germaine, Anna Müller, and Camille. To avoid confusion, I have minimized references to Virginia Hall's aliases and have relied primarily on her "true name" to tell her story.

CONTENTS

PART FOUR: THE CIA

VIRGINIA HALL'S WAR

I felt very much that it was my war as well
as my friends' war.

—Virginia Hall

On a March evening in 1944, a boat pulled out of an English harbor, heading across the English Channel to Nazi-occupied France. On board was Virginia Hall, an American from a prominent Baltimore, Maryland, family and only days away from her thirty-eighth birthday. She was placing her life at great risk by returning to France, where Virginia was well known as a spy. One British intelligence officer would later say of her, "From my point of view and that of many of my colleagues, Virginia Hall can be considered the greatest wartime agent."

As the boat left the English harbor, Virginia and her colleague—code-named Aramis—went on deck, where they observed three British patrol vessels following them. The boats tested their machine guns and antiaircraft guns on rocks laying outside the harbor—a sobering reminder

Self portrait of Virginia in a mirror.

that they were about to enter a war zone. After several hours of uncomfortable sleep, they were rousted out of their bunks at around 3:00 a.m. to prepare for their landing in France.

Fortunately, the sea was calm as two small boats were lowered over the side of the vessel. Each boat contained four men—three to row and a British officer armed with a Thompson submachine gun—to accompany Virginia and Aramis to shore. They rowed in silence. They could barely see the outline of the cliffs in the darkness as they approached the beach. Finally, they heard the crunch of stones as the boats slid onto the shore of Brittany in the early morning. Everyone quickly jumped out of the boats, where two men and two women waited to assist them. The bags were gathered up, and the party walked uphill on cobblestones.

As her adventure began, Virginia was determined to meet the challenges she knew were waiting for her.

ONE

A SPY IN TRAINING

I must have liberty, withal as large a charter as I please.

—Virginia Hall's quote upon graduation
from Roland Park Country School,
paraphrasing a quote from William
Shakespeare's *As You Like It*,
Act II, Scene 7

CHAPTER 1

THE FIGHTING BLADE

$\mathcal{V}$irginia Hall was born in Baltimore, Maryland, on April 6, 1906. Her grandfather, John W. Hall, stowed away on one of his father's clipper ships when he was nine years old. John would later become the master of a ship engaged with the China trade. He would go on to make his fortune in Baltimore as president of the Gas and Electric Company and president of the First National Bank. John's son, Edwin "Ned" Lee Hall, was Virginia's father. He had banking interests and owned several movie houses

Baby Virginia in her mother's lap.

Young Virginia and her brother, John, with flowers.

in Baltimore. Ned married his secretary, Barbara Virginia Hammel.

Virginia's only sibling was her brother, John, who was four years older. Family lore had it that in their childhood years, John mispronounced Virginia's name, calling her "Dindy," and the nickname stuck. They were a close-knit family.

The Halls had an apartment in Baltimore, but Edwin and Barbara purchased a country home outside of Baltimore—Box Horn Farm—in Parkton, Maryland. Their house in the country was a welcome respite from the city, particularly in the hot summer months. The farmhouse had plumbing but no central heating until after World War II, so it was most comfortable during the spring and summer. There were woodstoves and fireplaces to provide warmth during cold weather.

In order to satisfy the children's curiosity, the home's library was filled with books. The farm had over one hundred acres and was looked

The family home at Box Horn Farm.

after by a tenant farmer who worked the property for the family. A train, called the Parkton Local, ran regularly between Baltimore and Parkton, and it made the commute easy for Edwin to attend to his business interests in Baltimore. During some parts of the school year, Virginia would also take the commuter train from the farm to her school in Baltimore.

Virginia with pigeons.

Virginia and John loved spending time on the farm. There were hills, orchards, and woods to play in, and the two learned to hunt and fish. The barn was home to horses, goats, chickens, and cows.

Young Virginia riding piggyback on John.

Handling farm animals would later become valuable to Virginia in ways she could not have imagined during her childhood. Looking back at her time there, Virginia once reminded her niece, Lorna Catling, how important it was to learn everything you can. She remarked that "learning to milk the cows for fun turned out to be very handy."

Virginia and John (left and middle) on the farm.

In 1912, six-year-old Virginia Hall began attending the prestigious Roland Park Country School in Baltimore, where she immediately distinguished herself. Virginia loved sports and was an excellent athlete, playing tennis and baseball and going on to become captain of the school's varsity basketball and field hockey teams. She also enjoyed acting in the school's theatrical productions—where she sometimes portrayed male characters, a necessity in the all-girls' school.

Virginia also became editor in chief of *Quid Nunc*, the school's yearbook, and was elected president of her senior class. Virginia's profile in her senior yearbook stated:

> The "Donna Juanita" of the class now approaches. Though professing to hold Man in contempt, Dindy is yet his closest counterpart—in costume. She is, by her own confession, cantankerous and capricious, but in spite of it all we would not do without her; for she is our class-president, the editor-in-chief of this book, and one of the mainstays of the basket-ball and hockey teams. She has been acclaimed the most original of our class, and she lives up to her reputation at all times. The one thing to expect from Dind is the unexpected.

Virginia (right) playing a man in a costume drama at Roland Park Country School.

Virginia (standing, second from right) and her teammates on the 1924 girls' varsity basketball team at Roland Park Country School.

Young Virginia at Box Horn Farm.

One of Virginia's classmates would later recall that "there was a different manner about her. She was not a typical school girl. She was low key, rather than isolated. She was tall, big-boned and striking, but not in a conventional way. She kept her own counsel but was a definite presence."

Once, Virginia went to school wearing a live garter snake wrapped around her wrist as a bracelet. Self-confident and seemingly fearless, the school's ninth graders nicknamed her "The Fighting Blade." From an early age, it was clear that Virginia was destined to leave her mark on the world.

STUDENT OF EUROPE

*A*fter graduating from high school, Virginia went to college to pursue her restless intellectual curiosity, as well as her desire for adventure and travel. She attended Radcliffe College (which later merged with Harvard College) in Cambridge, Massachusetts, for the 1924–25 school year. She majored in economics, with a minor in foreign languages. She then transferred to Barnard College in New York for the 1925–26 academic year. But Virginia was impatient with these prestigious schools because she wasn't able to take the courses she wanted without taking what she considered to be "a lot of uninteresting required courses."

Virginia's sympathetic father encouraged her to pursue her academic interests in Europe, where she spent a year at the École des Sciences Politiques in Paris, France, studying economics and history. She then spent two years in Vienna, Austria, where she studied economics and international law at the Konsular

Virginia's father, Ned.

Akademie and graduated in June 1929. During her college years, she spent summers studying at the French Universities of Strasbourg, Grenoble, and Toulouse. Virginia also took courses at the American University in Washington, DC, during the 1929–30 academic year, as well as additional courses in French at the George Washington University in Washington, DC.

Virginia's extensive travel and study in Europe gave her the opportunity to learn more about the politics, history, and culture of the continent. Her extended residence in Europe, along with immersive language study, made her fluent in French, Italian, and German, though natives could often tell Virginia was a foreign speaker. She also picked up enough Spanish and Russian language skills to make herself understood where those languages were spoken.

Virginia's education and early experiences prepared her for a career in espionage. Prospective spies can be sent to school to learn about foreign languages and cultures, self-defense, firearms and munitions training, and espionage tradecraft such as surveillance and covert communications. But getting through "spy school" is no guarantee that the student of espionage will be successful.

No single quality guarantees success as a spy, especially in such a specialized and dangerous line of work where exposure—particularly during wartime—can mean imprisonment, torture, and execution. But by the time Virginia had completed her formal education, she had displayed the qualities that would suggest great potential for becoming a successful spy: She was smart with broad intellectual interests; she had an interest in, and skill with, European languages, history, and culture; she was observant; she exhibited leadership; she was self-confident; she

Young Virginia next to a lake.

had courage; she was willing to take risks but without being reckless or irresponsible; she was focused and determined; she demonstrated an ability to play different roles convincingly as an actress; she was adventurous; she had a love of the outdoors; and she was athletic.

Virginia would draw on these and other attributes for the rest of her life. But she would later say that all you really needed to be successful in espionage was common sense. And common sense was something that Virginia Hall had in abundance.

STATE DEPARTMENT YEARS

*V*irginia once said that the only way for a woman to get ahead at the time was to have plenty of money or her own business. But Virginia knew herself and characteristically decided to take an independent path by pursuing a public service career in government. Specifically, Virginia wanted to live abroad and work in the State Department. It was her goal to become a member of the professional diplomatic service as a Foreign Service Officer.

In August 1931, Virginia began her career as a civil servant, rather than a diplomat, in the State Department as a clerk making $2,500 per year. Her first posting was at the US Embassy in Warsaw, Poland. Her other overseas duty stations were Izmir (formerly known as Smyrna), Turkey; Venice, Italy; and Tallinn, Estonia. As a State Department clerk, Virginia's duties included translation; filing; visa and citizenship work; welfare; and reporting on economic, political, and financial issues.

While she was living in Europe, Virginia fell in love with a Polish army officer. The two seemed to be heading toward marriage, but then things ended. This was not the first time that Virginia had come close to being married. Earlier, when she was attending college in the United States, Virginia was involved with a man in Maryland. The couple was serious, but Virginia found out that he had been unfaithful to her, and she ended the relationship.

When Virginia was working at the US Consulate in Turkey, an incident occurred that would change her life forever. In the swamps outside Izmir, Virginia and several friends were hunting snipe, a game bird commonly found in marshy areas. While Virginia was experienced with firearms, she had her gun pointed down, and somehow it slipped. When she grabbed for it, she accidentally hit the trigger with her finger. The gun went off, causing serious damage to her left foot. By the time Virginia's friends got her to a hospital, septicemia, or blood poisoning, had set in. In order to save Virginia's life, it was decided that her left leg had to be amputated below the knee. An American surgeon rushed from Istanbul to Izmir to perform the operation.

Teenage Virginia holding a rifle.

It wasn't certain that Virginia would survive her injury. One night at the hospital, while she was fading in and out of consciousness, Virginia had a remarkable experience that she would recount over the course of her life. She said that her father, who had died in January 1931, visited her in the hospital room. He scooped her out of bed and held her in his lap in a rocking chair to talk to her. He told his beloved daughter that if the pain she was experiencing was too awful, she should simply let go; otherwise, her mother needed her.

That was a turning point. Virginia soon got better. She returned to her mother's home in Maryland to heal, was fitted for a prosthetic limb, and learned to walk again.

Virginia never allowed her disability to define her in any way.

Virginia and her friend Angelo in Venice, Italy.

The loss of her leg was just something Virginia dealt with, and she kept moving forward. Within the year, she returned to Europe and the State Department, resuming her clerical duties.

Virginia soon became dissatisfied with being a clerk, and she continued to apply unsuccessfully for a career in the State Department's Foreign Service. Virginia believed that she may have been discriminated against because of her artificial leg. While serving in the US Consulate in Venice, Italy, Virginia asked her friend Frank Egerton Webb for help.

Webb in turn appealed to his influential friend Colonel Edward M. House on behalf of Virginia. He characterized her as "a thorough gentlewoman of great intelligence." Webb told House that despite

Virginia leaning over a canal in Venice, Italy.

having an artificial leg, Virginia "walks without lameness, rows and swims and rides a horse." He noted that "she was then told that she would never rise any higher owing to the loss of her leg."

Colonel House, a prominent former diplomat and advisor to President Woodrow Wilson, in turn

President Roosevelt on the porch at Top Cottage in Hyde Park, New York, in 1941, with Ruthie Bie and Fala.

wrote then-President Franklin D. Roosevelt on January 31, 1938, citing Webb's concerns about discrimination against Virginia because of her disability. House told President Roosevelt, "if anything can be done in reference to Miss Hall, both he and I will appreciate it. It certainly seems unfair to bar Miss Hall from advancement for such a cause."

President Roosevelt, himself disabled because of polio and who generally used a wheelchair, was sympathetic to Virginia's situation. "Why, Oh, Why do the regulations governing entrance into the career service prescribe that amputation of any portion of a limb, except fingers or toes, disqualify the applicant?" an indignant Roosevelt wrote to his secretary of state, Cordell Hull, on February 9, 1938.

It seems to me that a regulation of this kind is a great mistake because it might exclude a first class applicant who had an artificial hand or an artificial leg and was perfectly capable of performing all Diplomatic Corps duties. After all, the Diplomatic Corps does not call for gymnasts; it does not have to climb trees, and I have known many people with wooden legs who dance just as well as many diplomats do who have natural legs.

President Roosevelt concluded his letter to Secretary of State Hull about Virginia (using a term for people with disabilities common at the time but now considered derogatory): "I feel deeply about it because cripples ought not to be penalized in the Government service if they are capable of performing their work. F.D.R."

In his response to the president, Secretary of State Hull denied that the State Department's regulations rigidly excluded individuals from serving in the Foreign Service as long as a physical disability did not "seriously interfere with his official performance." The State

President Roosevelt and Secretary of State Cordell Hull in Hyde Park, New York.

Department's Personnel Board and Medical Board had the discretion to consider situations on a case-by-case basis. Specifically regarding Virginia's application to the Foreign Service, Hull went on to tell the president:

> . . . I have considered the case of Miss Virginia Hall, who was the subject of the correspondence which occasioned your comment. I find that Miss Hall's record as a clerk in the Foreign Service has not been such as to commend her to the Personnel Board for appointment into the career Service, although her services in a clerical capacity cannot be termed unsatisfactory. It was undoubtedly this consideration, along with her physical disability, which was in mind when the instruction was drafted informing her that her application for designation to take the examination could not be approved . . .

Hull offered faint praise of Virginia in his letter to the president when he stated that "her services in a clerical capacity cannot be termed unsatisfactory," but he failed to elaborate on specifically what it was in her clerical role that "has not been such as to commend her to the Personnel Board for appointment into the career Service" other than "her physical disability." The secretary of state simply assured the president that Virginia was not being discriminated against solely because of her physical

Virginia's Estonian ID.

disability. Her appeal had gone to the secretary of state as well as the president of the United States, and that appeared to be the end of the matter. The door to advancement in a career position was apparently closed.

Discouraged, Virginia transferred from Venice in 1938 to continue performing clerical work at the US Consulate in Tallinn, Estonia.

With war clouds gathering over Europe, and facing the harsh reality that she didn't have a future in the State Department, in April 1939, Virginia resigned. At the time, the State Department offered to pay the expenses of its employees to return to the United States for up to one year from the date of resignation. Virginia decided to stay in Europe while she figured out what to do next with her life.

As the 1930s came to a close, Europe had become a powder keg, just waiting to be ignited. While Virginia was still in Estonia, the match was lit on September 1, 1939, when German forces invaded Poland. Two days later, France and Great Britain declared war on Germany. World War II had begun.

Virginia playing chess outside.

Virginia left Tallinn on October 25, 1939, and arrived in France on January 18, 1940. It was unclear what role Virginia would play in this terrifying new world, but she knew she wanted to be involved and help if she could.

CHAPTER 4

THE GATHERING STORM

With a broader conflict across Europe all but certain, Virginia was determined to do her part. From the outset, she was willing to place herself in harm's way in defense of freedom. In February 1940, Virginia, without first informing her family, joined a French ambulance unit attached to the Ninth Artillery Regiment. Her disability was apparently no obstacle to being accepted by the French Army. Hostilities in Europe reached a new level in April, when Germany attacked Norway and Denmark.

On May 6, 1940, Virginia moved up to a forward station at Droitaumont about twenty miles from Metz, in northeast France, close to the German border. Several days later on May 10, German forces invaded Luxembourg, Belgium, the Netherlands, and France. Around this time, Virginia sent a letter to her mother stating that she was living in a cottage and that there was "plenty of

Maryland Woman Is Driving Ambulance For French Army

Miss Virginia Hall Joined Allies Last February Without Telling Family Of Intentions

Somewhere in France, possibly in the farflung battle zone, there is a Maryland woman, an alumna of the Roland Park Country School, driving an ambulance for the French artillery.

She is Miss Virginia Hall, 33, whose grandfather was Capt. John W. Hall, president of the Gas and Electric Company and president of the First National Bank, and whose great-uncle, Robert C. Hall, was president of the Maryland Jockey Club.

Miss Hall's mother, Mrs. Edwin L. Hall, of Box Horn Farm, Parkton, Baltimore county, last night disclosed her daughter's whereabouts. The mother revealed that she was anxiously awaiting word from her daughter, since she has had no letter since one in May that said only that Miss Hall was at the front, "weary and grubby" but "well taken care of."

"These words were well-intentioned,", Mrs. Hall said, "but they afford me little consolation, for in her characteristic manner she is trying to make things sound better for me."

Mrs. Hall said that her daughter joined the French ambulance unit—

(Continued on Page 6, Column 2)

The Baltimore Sun *reports on Virginia's work as an ambulance driver for the French Army.*

good food." Virginia reported that she was at the front, "weary and grubby" but "well taken care of."

In an interview with a reporter from the *Baltimore Sun* in June 1940, Virginia's mother stated that she was anxiously awaiting further word from her daughter, whom she hadn't heard from since that letter in early May. Virginia's remarks in that letter did not reassure her mother. "These words were well-intentioned," Mrs. Hall told the reporter, "but they afford me little consolation, for in her characteristic manner she is trying to make things sound better for me."

Great Britain's government urged France to continue the fight against Hitler's forces, but France's leadership sued for peace. On June 16, 1940, two days after German forces occupied Paris, the elderly Marshal Henri-Philippe Pétain, a military hero of World

Adolf Hitler in front of the Eiffel Tower a few weeks after the German occupation began.

War I, became prime minister of France. His first responsibility was to initiate truce negotiations with the Germans. On June 22, the two countries signed an armistice that divided France into a northern zone controlled by the German Army, and a southern zone administered by Pétain's government and located in the resort town of Vichy. Some thought of Pétain as the country's savior in a time of grave national emergency. However, many others thought of Pétain as a traitor to France and the leader of an oppressive, authoritarian regime that supported the German war effort, as well as the Nazis' brutal persecution of Jews.

Virginia was in Paris when France surrendered to Germany on June 22, 1940. She would later say that "at the time of defeat we all felt nothing but fury." Virginia eventually wrangled an exit visa from France and went by train through Spain to Lisbon, Portugal, and then took a plane to England on September 1, 1940.

Hitler salute in Vichy, France.

Pétain and his regime in Vichy made the complete military occupation of France unnecessary. The Germans exploited the French, shipping trainloads of food and other products back to Germany. This in turn created massive food shortages and required rationing for the demoralized French population. Approximately 1.8 million French prisoners of war (POWs) were held in Germany and fighting with the Germans resulted in roughly three hundred thousand dead or seriously injured French citizens.

The people of France paid a high price for Pétain's peace agreement with Nazi Germany. Their living standards declined, and they lost their democratic rights. Vichy France became a police state and a willing accomplice in the Holocaust, and anyone who opposed the new regime was persecuted. The Nazi occupation of France was particularly jarring in Paris, one of the most beautiful cities in the world. Buildings were covered with swastikas,

German soldiers in front of the Paris opera house.

French Maquis guerrillas in the mountains.

German road signs were visible throughout the city, and Hitler's soldiers seemed to be everywhere. French citizens who actively supported and cooperated with the Vichy government became known as collaborators.

Many young Frenchmen, facing the prospect of forced labor in Germany, took to the hills in France. They became natural recruits to fight against Vichy and the Nazis. Ultimately, many of them turned to the Resistance—anyone who fought against German or Vichy rule in France—to provide them with food and shelter.

The rural guerrilla bands of French Resistance fighters were known as the Maquis, and the individual fighters were referred to as maquisards. Many of them were working-class young men under the age of twenty-five, representing a broad spectrum of political affiliations. They became more effective organizationally as the war went on.

Despite the fact that France had become a police state, many citizens had no desire to collaborate with the German invaders. It was important for them to do what they could to resist the new regime. In a famous speech delivered on June 18, 1940, French general Charles de Gaulle proclaimed himself leader of the French government-in-exile. In a BBC radio broadcast to his countrymen, he called on them to resist the German invaders. He stated:

I, General de Gaulle, now in London, call upon the French officers and soldiers who are or who may find themselves on British soil, with or without their weapons, I call upon the engineers and the skilled workers in the armaments industry who are or who may find themselves on British soil, to join me. Whatever happens, the flame of French resistance must not and shall not die. Tomorrow, as today, I shall speak on the radio from London.

Outside of France, de Gaulle became the most prominent of the *résistants*, as they were known.

Many French citizens listened to the BBC radio broadcasts—a violation of law in the new order. These broadcasts included a nightly news program in French, as well as brief segments for "Free French," which helped make de Gaulle the embodiment of opposition to the Vichy regime.

Adolescent members of the French Resistance marching with their weapons drawn.

But the *résistants* who took the greatest risks were those who lived in France. A scholar of the Resistance characterized its members as "ordinary people, who were angry, humiliated or ashamed, or all three at the same time, decided to change things, despite the fact that they had neither the experience nor the means to make things happen. They had the will, and that was enough." The Resistance took many forms, from writing slogans on walls, to producing and distributing underground news-papers, to committing various acts of sabotage. All these activities were dangerous.

Being a member of the secret army of the Resistance in

some ways posed greater risks for the *résistants* than it did for uniformed soldiers in the regular army. If the uniformed military was captured by the enemy, certain protections were afforded them under military codes of warfare. But members of the Resistance, wearing civilian clothing, could only operate effectively if they were undetected. They were isolated, underfunded or with no resources at all, and often didn't have any weapons or other military equipment. And they constantly lived under the tremendous stress of being discovered and betrayed, which in turn would have led to almost certain imprisonment, torture, and even execution.

Some experts estimate that no more than five hundred thousand French citizens—or less than 2 percent of the French population—were involved in the Resistance. Of that number, approximately one hundred thousand were thought to have died during World War II: killed in combat, executed, or died while imprisoned. The Resistance groups were unified in their commitment to fighting the occupation, yet it was sometimes a challenge to get so many different groups unified in specific actions against the Nazis and the Vichy regime. But the lack of coordination among these small groups also added to their security when members were betrayed, and fewer members were at risk when someone was compromised. This was the challenging environment in which Virginia Hall and others would have to operate.

CHAPTER 5

WARTIME LONDON: WEARING LIFE LIKE A LOOSE GARMENT

When Virginia arrived in wartime London in September 1940, she was fortunate to get a job at the US Embassy. At a salary of $1,200 a year, she was employed as a code clerk and accountant, where her duties included handling confidential codes for Raymond Lee, a general in the United States Army who was serving as the US military attaché and head of intelligence in London.

Virginia began her job at the embassy during a particularly tumultuous time. Hitler's forces had defeated France and much of Western Europe. Great Britain stood alone. The United States had not yet entered the war, and the British knew that American support would be key to their national survival.

Hitler was furious at the British Royal Air Force (RAF) for bombing German cities, and he became determined to destroy

An underground station converted into a shelter in London's West End during the Blitz.

the British capital city and break the will of the people. In early September 1940, the German air force, or Luftwaffe, began a massive bombing campaign against London and other British cities in an effort both to defeat British morale and

Virginia sitting at table.

draw the RAF into destructive battles. This unprecedented air attack against British civilian targets became known as the Blitz.

Virginia provided support to General Lee, who was a highly capable and sophisticated intelligence specialist. Additionally, he liked and understood the British, and was sympathetic to their plight but was ever mindful of America's official neutrality in the conflict.

Lee was also an astute observer of life in London during this bleak period. Virginia inhabited this same world. Lee dutifully recorded the great reduction in traffic, the fact that most men—and many women—were wearing military uniforms, the need to carry identification and ration cards at all times, and that many Londoners were carrying gas masks. Lights were cut off or shaded after sunset on threat of fines or imprisonment. Food was heavily rationed, and "one gets only a lump of sugar and a thin little flake of butter." Junk metal was extensively salvaged for the war effort. No one was permitted on the beaches, which were covered with barbed wire emplacements to prevent a potential German invasion. And no radios were allowed in cars.

A few days after Hitler unleashed the Blitz, General Lee commented that "if there was ever a time when one should wear life like a loose garment, this is it." He saw the frightening assault on London firsthand, as did Virginia, but kept the destruction in perspective. After one Nazi raid, he commented, "A really large amount of damage was done last night. But none of it was vital. It is all of it, or nearly all, just aimless, random battering. To hell with Hitler, I say."

Prime Minister Winston Churchill inspects German bombing damage to London's East End.

The brutality of the London Blitz increased American sympathy to the plight of Great Britain, and a growing number of Americans saw the necessity of fighting the Nazi threat. Undoubtedly, Virginia Hall felt the same way. Only five months after she began her position in the US Embassy in London, her wartime service took a new direction as she decided to risk everything to become a spy for the British.

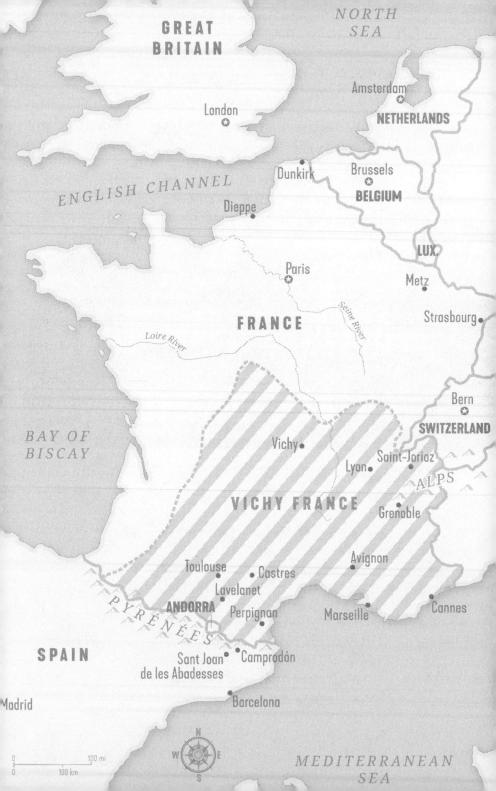

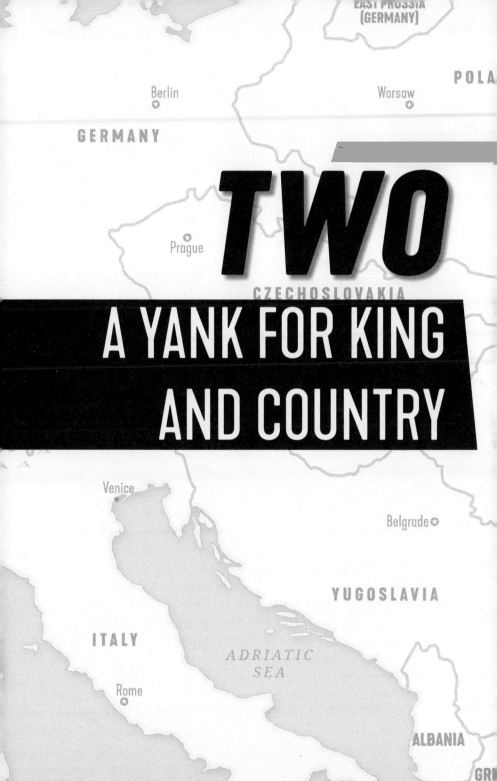

TWO

A YANK FOR KING AND COUNTRY

THE NEW RECRUIT

*W*hen France collapsed, the United States was still not involved in the war. Great Britain had only the English Channel standing between it and continental Europe, which was largely under the control of Nazi Germany. Since the British Army had been pushed out of continental Europe, the island nation had to determine how it could best fight Hitler. They ultimately decided on a three-part strategy: strategic aerial bombing, a naval blockade, and undermining German rule in occupied nations through sabotage and subversion.

On July 19, 1940, Adolf Hitler delivered a speech in Berlin boasting of his government's military victories and predicting Great Britain's defeat. That same day, in a memorandum to his war cabinet, Prime Minister Winston Churchill announced the creation of the Special Operations Executive (SOE). The new organization was to "co-ordinate all actions by way of subversion and sabotage against the enemy overseas." Efforts at subversion were intended to foster popular discontent, if not revolt against the occupiers.

The organization sought to destroy or damage trains, bridges, factories, and other facilities that were important to the enemy, as well as to collect information on the enemy's intentions and capabilities. This covert activity was led or supported by SOE agents in occupied countries such as France, Albania, Belgium, and Greece. The SOE also had a branch focused on Asia. Its agents were dropped behind enemy lines by parachute, or brought ashore by submarines or small boats. Churchill's directive to the secretive new organization was simple and straightforward: "And now set Europe ablaze." The organization was divided into different sections, focusing on different countries.

The component of the SOE dealing with France, or F Section as it was known, would ultimately build up almost a hundred circuits—networks of subversive agents—in France. They

French Resistance fighters sabotaging a railway in Saône-et-Loire.

would arm thousands of French members of the Resistance. The SOE's circuits had code names such as Spindle, Tinker, Wheelwright, Stockbroker, Author, and Marksman. Over 100 of the approximately 450 agents the SOE sent to France did not survive the war.

The core of the SOE's circuits were three-person teams, each of which played a distinct role. The team leader was an organizer who was responsible for planning and recruiting individuals to the Resistance. The courier traveled among the other members of the team and members of the Resistance, transporting messages, funds, equipment, and weaponry. Because many men were absent from the home front, women were less conspicuous traveling throughout the country and often served as couriers.

The third member of the team was the wireless telegraph, or W/T, operator who would send coded messages to London related to agents, supply drops, and other important information regarding the operational environment on the ground. Keeping in contact with London was essential for the circuits to accomplish their missions. The W/T operator was burdened with one or two suitcases of heavy equipment and the threat of being detected by German forces on the lookout for Resistance communications. German listening stations would pick up a signal and then vans or German forces on foot would arrive at the source of the transmission.

These wireless telegraph operators took tremendous risks and were under enormous pressure to keep their messages short to avoid detection. By the middle of 1943, the average wireless telegraph operator in France was arrested after only six weeks of doing their job.

Recruiting the right individuals to perform these dangerous and important roles for the SOE was a high priority. The most sought after qualities for prospective agents were "a level head and steady nerves."

On Tuesday evening, January 14, 1941, Virginia had one of the more important encounters of her life. She was at a social gathering in London, and during the course of the evening, an SOE official developed more than a social interest in the thirty-four-year-old American who was working at the US Embassy. A priority was gauging Virginia's willingness to return to continental Europe.

The next day, the official reported to SOE colleagues that Virginia had talked of "wanting to go for about a month to France" via Lisbon, Portugal, or Barcelona, Spain. She also raised the possibility of working to assist refugees by "joining hands with the Quaker organization" in order to return to the mainland. Intrigued, the British intelligence official was careful not to push the issue with her. But the official was struck that this Baltimore native might be used in a mission for the British. Perhaps the SOE might wish to facilitate her trip to Lisbon and back, and pay her way "in exchange for what service she could render us."

In the parlance of spy recruitment, Virginia had been spotted, and now she was to be assessed. She was seen as an excellent candidate for recruitment to British intelligence. Nevertheless, there was a realization that they needed to get more details about her. The official pledged to "put her through the cards, at the same time continuing approaches with the same end in view."

After an initial assessment, British authorities scrutinized Virginia more closely to determine if she was suitable to become an intelligence officer. One month later, on February 14, 1941, it was recommended that Virginia be used "as a Class A Liaison in France—Unoccupied territory—with journalistic cover."

That same day, an "Enquiry for Information" regarding Miss Virginia Hall of 4 Queen Street, W1, London, was made to MI5—Great Britain's domestic counterintelligence and security agency charged with protecting the nation's secrets—to assess her suitability to be employed as a Class A Liaison in unoccupied France. British authorities were "running the traps" to make sure that Virginia was representing herself accurately and was not an agent of the Nazis or any other hostile nation. Just three days later, MI5 responded, "Nothing recorded against."

While the British were vetting Virginia, they also needed to develop a cover identity for her intelligence-gathering mission in Vichy France. A London correspondent for the daily newspaper *PM*, published in New York City, was approached to see if they would be willing to provide cover for Virginia as a correspondent for the newspaper in France. It was noted that Ralph Ingersoll, the owner and director of the paper, would ultimately have to give permission. The directive to British authorities was as follows:

Will you cause Ingersoll to be approached tactfully and find out whether he has any objection. Please make it clear that we are paying all expenses and that Miss Hall need only be paid space rates by him for any material used. She has journalistic experience.

The directive concluded with a clear and straightforward description of what British intelligence was expecting of Virginia in Vichy France: "Also please make it clear that we are not asking Miss Hall to do anything more than keep her eyes and ears open."

As the British committed themselves to working with Virginia, she formalized her own commitment to working with them. On May 14, 1941, Virginia Hall—a US citizen—signed the United Kingdom's Official Secrets Acts, promising to keep her work for the British secret and acknowledging the serious legal penalties for failing to do so.

The arrangement to have Virginia provided a cover story by *PM* apparently fell through, and Virginia would find another American sponsor for her espionage on behalf of the British. On May 21, 1941, an SOE official met with George Backer, the publisher of the *New York Post*, at Claridge's, an exclusive hotel in London. Backer handed the official an attestation that Virginia Hall was a fully accredited correspondent for the *Post*. The official noted that Backer, "without saying anything, was obviously aware of an ulterior motive" and supportive of helping provide a cover story for Virginia's activities in Vichy France. That same day, Virginia went to the American Embassy in London to obtain an extension of her US passport, along with authorization for travel through Portugal, Spain, and France.

On May 27, 1941, an SOE official saw Virginia, and she told him that the US Embassy and Consulate in England were quite willing to send a telegram pressing her application for a French visa from the Vichy government in France, but they had to obtain Washington's consent. But Washington refused, arguing that no special assistance should be given in the matter. Despite such administrative problems, Virginia was still being vetted. Before long, the SOE considered her a desirable recruit.

Virginia's preparation for her new assignment was relatively minimal. She recalled, "I was not trained by SOE before going to France except for a political briefing." Nor did Virginia receive any sabotage training from the British.

German and Vichy authorities considered women less likely to be intelligence agents, and therefore, the SOE was more inclined to use women in this role. Women were prominent in France during the occupation, traveling, shopping, and working in the place of absent husbands and other male family members. And as the United States had not yet entered the war at this stage, Virginia was allowed generally free movement around France.

Virginia with skis next to her car.

Virginia responded to questions from British intelligence about her parents, education background, and language skills. She stated that she was five feet, eight inches tall in her stocking feet, and weighed 138 pounds. She had made out her will. Her hair and eyes were brown. Her complexion was fair. Virginia also indicated that she could ride a horse, drive a car, swim, mountaineer, sail a boat, ski, shoot a firearm, and bicycle. She also stated that she could not run, fly an airplane, box, sketch, read or transmit Morse code, and had no knowledge of wireless radios. She described her religion as Episcopalian and considered herself best suited to working in the field of journalism. What political views did Virginia have? "None," she replied.

Virginia left for the field for her SOE mission in France on August 23, 1941. She flew from England to Lisbon, Portugal, and then took a flight from Lisbon to Barcelona, Spain, via Lufthansa, a German airline—an irony that delighted Virginia. The final leg of her journey, from Barcelona to Vichy, was taken by train. At last, Virginia was in France and ready to fight against tyranny.

CHAPTER 7

VIRGINIA'S INTELLIGENCE CIRCLE

*W*hen Virginia arrived in Vichy France, she established herself in the capital of unoccupied France and was the SOE's first female agent in the country. Once there, Virginia registered with the local gendarmerie, or military police, and established reliable contacts within the organization. She introduced herself as a new correspondent for the *New York Post*, while also living her clandestine life as an intelligence operative for the British. Virginia's mission was to collect information on the situation in France, while aiding the French Resistance. She was also supposed to look for ways to assist SOE agents, as well as British pilots and others, in escaping German and Vichy authorities— what was known as escape and evasion (E&E) activity.

Soon after arriving, Virginia moved to Lyon, where she set about organizing the SOE's Heckler circuit and operating

Virginia's journalist ID card.

out of her apartment at 3 Place Ollier. She took on a wide variety of activities, including advising SOE agents about crossing into German-occupied France and distributing radio transmitters to agents who passed along her reports to SOE headquarters in London, and she traveled extensively, meeting with other SOE agents.

Virginia was modest about the important and dangerous role she played as an intelligence operative in wartime France. "I was no heroine—I was there to help and back up the men who did the work; false papers, get them out, take care of trouble—my French friends did it all for me." Virginia took tremendous risks in this work, but as she noted, she also depended heavily on her "French friends" to get the job done. Several of these French patriots were particularly notable.

One of Virginia's most valuable and reliable colleagues, Dr. Jean Rousset of Lyon, a prominent gynecologist, came to work for her in November 1941. Virginia referred to him by a code name, Pepin. Initially, he served Virginia by providing a letter box for information coming from Paris. Later, relying on his own contacts in the Lyon area, he provided economic information to Virginia, such as the nature and extent of metals and minerals being exported to Germany from the Lyon area.

As a physician, Dr. Rousset tended to the health of agents who had become sick during their stay in the area. He offered nurses, doctors, and ambulances, and would place agents at his clinic when they desperately needed medical care. Virginia informed London that "he is most devoted to this good cause and quite willing to do anything for us."

For some of his medical cases, he provided medical certifications so they would not be conscripted into forced labor in Germany. Dr. Rousset also made arrangements with a small mental health clinic to place Virginia's sick agents there under false names so they could be cared for in security. Virginia said of him: "Dr. Rousset was and is always an ardent collaborator of [ours] and gave his help and time to the utmost and eventually his liberty."

Another important Resistance colleague of Virginia's, and one of the first to be willing to work with her, was Eugene Labourier. Virginia met him in December 1941 on a visit to Le Puy. At the time, Labourier was serving as *Ingenieur des Ponts et Chaussées*—engineer of bridges and roads—for the Haute-Loire Department of France. He promised to do what he could to help Virginia.

For example, in the spring of 1942, Virginia needed to transport political prisoners from a spot near Vichy to Châteauroux. Labourier provided trucks, one of which he drove. Later, he and several Resistance colleagues would go out at night to drop points in the Haute-Loire to gather supplies dropped by plane and use wheelbarrows to bring the material to hiding places. Labourier organized most of the men in this circuit, including nearly all the gendarmes in the district.

Madame Andre Michel, who was known as Maggy, was recruited in the spring of 1942 to serve as both a courier and a housekeeper for Monsieur Moran, known as Eugene. He was a radio operator for Virginia's circuit of agents operating in Lyon, passing along messages to and from London. Maggy left her apartment in Avignon to come to Lyon and take care of Eugene and served as a courier to him and Virginia. For security reasons, in August 1942 she and Eugene moved their operations to Avignon. Maggy continued her courier work, traveling between Lyon and Avignon every three or four days.

Maggy had a sister in Marseille who had a factory for making fine leather goods as well as a shop. It was suggested that an effective password for contacting her would be to inquire about "the flat out in the Armenian quarter of Marseille"—meaning her apartment that Virginia would be using.

Another friend and collaborator was Monsieur J. Joulian, who had worked with Virginia since December 1941. Joulian and his wife offered their home as a safe house, taking care of a number of agents and even allowing several wireless telegraph operators to work from their house—at considerable risk to themselves. Because he was exposed to poison gas during World War I, Monsieur Joulian was not in good health. Nevertheless, he continually took risks to help Virginia and the Resistance, serving as treasurer and recorder for the Resistance group operating in the Haute-Loire, and purchasing and storing food in case it was needed in an emergency.

One of Virginia's closest collaborators in Lyon was Germaine Guerin, whom she met in the winter of 1942. Germaine began to provide assistance to Virginia almost immediately, without even knowing the true nature of Virginia's work. Maurice Buckmaster, head of the SOE's F Section, characterized Germaine as "a woman of considerable attainments who incidentally works the Black Market, and is part owner of a brothel." Nevertheless, Germaine was totally committed to "working hard for what she calls 'the revolution against the German occupiers.'"

Virginia received information from many sources, and the prostitutes employed by Germaine had interesting and valuable insights from their intimate encounters with German soldiers and officials. In a letter to a friend, Virginia noted, "I've made some tart friends. They tell me their Jerry [a disparaging nickname for Germans] bed companions are not so bright as once was. In fact many are downright pessimistic. Excuse my acquaintances—but they know a hell of a lot!"

Germaine Guerin was responsible for keeping up a steady supply of food for the Resistance and those they were trying to help. Through her wide circle of contacts, she supplied the safe houses with both cooking and heating stoves and supplied coal to keep the flats warm during cold weather—a remarkable achievement in wartime France, where fuel and food were strictly rationed.

Germaine also provided clothing for escaped pilots and food for other Resistance members who were hiding in Lyon. In the summer of 1942, Virginia gave Germaine a somewhat better sense of her work supporting the Resistance, and asked Germaine for more consistent support. Germaine allowed Virginia to use three apartments as safe houses for agents visiting Lyon. During that summer, Virginia was often busy taking care of agents, or pilots on their way home.

On August 19, 1942, the Allies launched Operation Jubilee, the largest Allied raid on occupied Europe up until that time. Over six thousand troops, primarily Canadian, made an assault on Dieppe, a small port city on France's Normandy coast. However, in the face of superior German forces, the Dieppe raid proved a disaster for the Allies and made it clear that an Allied invasion of Europe would take substantially more time and preparation to be a success. Virginia helped arrange for the escape of three French

British and Canadian POWs, escorted at gunpoint by German troops, after the Dieppe assault.

Canadians from the raid who had been brought to her by a policeman. Germaine helped to take care of the men.

Virginia also worked with a pair of brothers. Alfred and Henry Newton were born ten years apart and

Members of the French Resistance listening to radio messages from London.

raised primarily in France. They became well known in Europe as cabaret artists—entertainers who gave dancing and singing performances in restaurants or nightclubs. After the outbreak of World War II, the two men formed one of the first underground movements in France's unoccupied zone, engaging in minor sabotage and passing along information they had received from monitoring BBC radio broadcasts from London on a hidden receiver. At the end of 1941, the brothers found out that their parents, wives, and Alfred's three children were killed when their ship taking them to safety in England was sunk by a German U-boat off the coast of Portugal. Devastated by the loss, the two men were determined to extract their revenge on the Germans.

When the brothers came to work for the SOE, Alfred was code-named Artus and Henry was code-named Auguste. Unofficially, London headquarters referred to them as "the twins." They were to be deployed in the Lyon area, where they were to instruct

Resistance members in sabotage and guerrilla tactics as well as how to handle British weapons.

To discreetly announce their deployment in France, in late June 1942, an evening BBC broadcast transmitted its list of coded messages to Resistance reception committees throughout France. One of the cryptic broadcast messages was *Les durs des durs arrivent*, which means "the toughest of the tough are arriving." The twins were on their way. Shortly thereafter, the two Newton brothers, along with their radio operator, Brian Stonehouse, code-named Célestin, were parachuted into central France.

After landing in France, the group was treated dismissively by the head of the circuit they were supposed to join. Despite this setback, the two men independently carved out a mission for themselves in the Lyon area, recruiting and training Resistance members, conducting sabotage, scouting suitable drop zones in the countryside, surveilling military facilities, and identifying sabotage targets. They soon formed their own circuit, called Greenheart. They got to know Virginia and provided her with French gendarme uniforms to help Resistance members escape the prison at Castres. For her part, Virginia did what she could to help "the twins," or as she affectionately referred to them, "the Siamese twins."

In the early summer of 1942, Madame Eugenie Catin of Lyon had been recruited to serve as a courier for "the Siamese twins," further placing herself at risk by providing them with a place to stay in Lyon when the brothers needed it. Virginia noted that she "did excellent work" as a courier and was "indefatigable in the question of rail travel, which at that time was most difficult and tiring."

Along with her numerous SOE and Resistance contacts, Virginia also encountered notable French officials. For instance, Virginia met with Raoul Dautry, a French politician, business leader, and engineer who was a prominent official in the French government prior to the German invasion of France. In a letter to London, Virginia reported that Dautry indicated that he wanted to escape occupied France. He had tried unsuccessfully to leave via Algiers in North Africa on two occasions, and he now wished to go to the United States. However, Dautry needed an invitation from an American university or foundation, as well as a supporting letter from France's embassy in Washington, DC. If he was successful, he would depart to America via London, giving the SOE an opportunity to consult with the Frenchman. Virginia's assessment—termed a "pious hope" by one of her SOE colleagues—was that there would be propaganda value in such a prominent individual leaving France. Ultimately, however, Dautry stayed in France for the duration of the war.

Virginia had other important contacts elsewhere in France. For example, in Marseille, her contacts primarily assisted prisoners of war in escaping. She had several good friends, Madame Landry in particular, who had connections in Paris and was able to assist refugees with fake ration and identity cards. These sources passed along verbal messages for Virginia, helping to keep her informed of Resistance activities throughout the country.

WARTIME FRANCE THROUGH A SPY'S EYES

*V*irginia dutifully lived her cover story that she was a reporter for the *New York Post*, writing a variety of articles about life in unoccupied Vichy France. That cover also gave her a valid justification for her travel around the country and allowed her to make firsthand observations about life in France that she could pass along to British intelligence. It also provided an opportunity to make the contacts necessary to accomplish her real work. Virginia's articles were a valuable insight into life in wartime France, as well as her operational environment as a spy.

In June 1942, Virginia submitted a story about the plight of European Jews and how they were being treated as second-class citizens under the new regime. She noted, "The Jews in Paris, meantime, are wearing the badge of their race—a five [*sic*] pointed yellow star." Another topic was the improvement in treatment of French prisoners in Germany, and how Vichy French officers took on some of the administrative duties of overseeing their countrymen in these camps. She had earlier noted that it was "a heavy responsibility for they must answer for each escape that takes place in their camp."

Virginia (right) in front of a statue in Europe with a woman and child.

Virginia also wrote about the Vichy government's appeal for scrap metal to support the nation's industry, and about the government's assurance, in the face of great skepticism, that "the metal collected will not go to the Reich."

Virginia also addressed more obscure aspects of French life in her articles for the *New York Post*, including the imposition of harsher measures against counterfeiters; the Vichy regime's efforts to reactivate its economic coordination with the continent; and a woman and her daughter traveling to the "Forbidden Zone" in northern France, which was occupied by the Germans. Virginia even wrote about the return to France of mange, a contagious skin disease caused by parasitic mites.

A covert intelligence officer wasn't immune to maladies though. As Virginia wrote a friend, "I still retain my rotundity, shingles. It isn't really shingles. It's 'lichen' [any of several skin diseases] a purely nervous disease says the doc. I hope he's not kidding as it's g.d. awful looking—anyhow it isn't mange."

In April 1942, Virginia discussed how French morale seemed particularly low. She observed that "the French have got the habit of meekly accepting during the past year. They have accepted stricter and stricter rations, lessening of rations, restrictions on wine, less bread, less alcohol, no beer, until finally they have arrived at the state of eating rutabaga for supper, washed down with mineral water—no beer or wine is served in the evening with meals (or without for the most part) meekly and without a murmur. It is incredible but true."

She expanded on this theme in an October 1941 article entitled "Odd Bits," in which Virginia talked about how the war had caused the people of France to change their ways and customs. "Everybody eats less than before, of course; most people wear less." She added, "whether morals will snap back once the situation returns to normal or not is the question. For the present, practically everyone is cherishing and condoning dishonesty in some degree."

Virginia went on to describe her recent living situation. While her comments would appear to be lighthearted observations for her readers, they provide a glimpse into how challenging her secret life as a covert agent must have been, constantly on the search for obscure places to conduct her operations:

I have been living for the past week in a convent of clois-tered nuns on the verdant hillside rising from the Saône, just above its juncture with the Rhone. Change for me—I have to be in at 6:30 p.m.! But Lyon is so crowded with refugees from the north and south who have taken up temporary residence there that it is all but impossible to find a place to live. A couple hundred thousand extra in a town of some five hundred seventy thousand cre-ated a proper congestion as to the housing problem. So, the hotels having turned me down for lack of room, the Sisters kindly took me in and gave me a tiny room in a square tower at one end of the convent up on the hill, where I have a most magnificent view over the city and up the river, and the undivided attention of a strong north wind. We lunch at 10 a.m., sup at 5 p.m. and the gates close at 6:30 p.m.—certainly a change to my pre-war existence in France. However, I have to thank present conditions for my introduction to these Sisters who have shown me such hospitality and kindness.

The nuns had a small farm on the convent, and Virginia reported that some milk and butter had been stolen recently. But the sisters were philosophical about the thefts: "What can you expect? People are hungry."

Virginia observed that the quest for food was an understand-able obsession for the French at a time of great scarcity. Fishing, for example, had become "a serious matter":

It has changed from a sport to a means to an end. The end being dinner—God willing. Waiting in the electric [trolley car] on the side of the [Saône] the other day I was fascinated by a cheery gent with a cherry nose, a very bright eye and a lively tongue who had spread at his feet on the platform by the side of the car some black moist earth on newspapers. "Worms, worms," he cried, "Nice, fine, dainty worms, come and get 'em." And they did! It was Saturday and lots of men were heading for the tram with their bundles of rods and creel on their shoulders. Some stopped right away and had a nickel's worth. Others—apparently superior—paid no attention to the luring: "luscious worms fit for the fastidious! Messieurs, have a worm!" But one old chap got in the car, sat down ahead of me, looked out the window at the worm man for a bit, then couldn't bear it any longer and out he went. He came back with a most stained little bundle of black earth and red "dainty" worms. Another fisherman across the aisle engaged him in conversation. I listened and learned. "Fine but solid that's the secret of fishing." "Ah, the days when we used horsehair. Now that was something like!" (Why should horsehair disappear from a conquered country?) "He gets them in the gutters in the suburbs. In fact he has two or three others gathering worms and he does the selling." "They're fine ones too, and hard to get now!" (Do even worms disappear with occupation?) About this time the electric pulled out and

I looked back at the cheerful seller of worms, who was calling out: "Worms, gentlemen, worms. I've been collecting them since five this morning just for you. Lovely worms. Come and get 'em!"

People lining up at a grocery store in a small French town in hopes of getting groceries during the food shortage.

As part of her work as an undercover intelligence agent for SOE, Virginia traveled a great deal: meeting fellow agents, members of the Resistance, and their supporters; scouting fields for airdrops; and assessing and acquiring safe houses in which to conceal individuals fleeing the Germans and Vichy authorities. When she wrote about her travel experiences, it was also an insight into the challenges facing an intelligence agent in unoccupied France.

Of one trip in unoccupied France, Virginia noted that "travel is no longer a pleasure but a grim undertaking not to be embarked upon lightly. It is devastating for the weak and exhausting even for the strong. Trains are crowded beyond belief and look like a Walt Disney brainstorm, with passengers filling all the windows of compartments and corridors alike and packed into the entrance platforms so that often the doors cannot close."

Because of the war, train service was sharply curtailed, with trains departing "at discouragingly inconvenient hours" in the early morning or in the late evening, making connections extremely challenging. There was little travel by either private automobile or bus because of a lack of fuel. This tended, she noted, "to suppress all but the most imperative travel." But even travel for business or urgent family reasons caused the few available trains to be filled to overflowing with passengers. It was often a battle to squeeze oneself onto a crowded train. Virginia observed, through firsthand experience, that "it's dismal to be left on the platform, ticket in hand, all dressed up and no place to go."

With secondary railway lines being largely eliminated, travel to the countryside was dependent on buses that ran sporadically, were poorly serviced because of wartime shortages, and therefore frequently broke down. Because of the overall unreliability of transportation, Virginia argued that "one should not expect to make a connection, but to spend the night at the connecting point and get the next day's conveyance, road or rail and then, if by chance you can and do make a close connection, it is truly cause for triumphant rejoicing."

On another occasion, Virginia made a brief trip to the Midi, or southern, region of France "to see the countryside." The first part of the trip was on a crowded bus. She stayed overnight at

Avignon, planning to take a bus to Marseille, which only ran once a day, leaving Avignon at 9:00 a.m. Virginia rose early and was at the station at 8:00 a.m. in the hope of being able to get a seat. Other prospective passengers had the same idea and were already waiting when Virginia arrived, and more came as they awaited the bus.

When the bus finally pulled into the station at 8:30 a.m., Virginia was squashed by the crowd surging to get on. The driver tried to bring order to the chaos by asking that the first to board be those with priority tickets (e.g., those who were ill or wounded). Then, those who were going farthest on the trip were to get in next. The result was that Virginia was relegated to standing in the back of a bus that was crowded with other standing passengers.

By 9:00 a.m., the bus was crammed with passengers, and bicycles, baby carriages, and a wide array of baggage were piled on top of the vehicle. The bus then took off for four long, hot hours lumbering along the dusty Midi road. Several hours into the trip, one of the men standing next to Virginia said to his companion, "Eh, old chap, I think our partridges are a bit dear this year."

Astonished, Virginia said to him, "You think of going shooting after this trip?"

"That is what we're going for," he replied with a grin. "The larder's pretty empty, you know, and I have a daughter in Marseille who needs food. It will be precious game she gets, if any. Still, it's needed." Virginia and the man continued their conversation until she finally got off the bus, and she bid farewell to her travel companions.

After the first leg of her trip, Virginia had to stay over in the local town for several days because of infrequent bus service and the crowding on the few buses that were operating. Finally, after three days, she was one of three people to get on a bus, but it was "standing room only." She said of the experience, "I was beginning to learn and to appreciate the difficulties under which France and her people are laboring."

When the bus reached the next town on the way to Marseille, two or three more passengers came aboard. A tremendous amount of freight, however, was added to the top of the bus: "baskets of grapes, sacks of vegetables, a wicker basket with a chicken in it, a baby carriage, boxes, crates, bags, suitcases."

Witnessing the produce that went on top of the bus gave Virginia greater appreciation of the food shortages experienced in French urban centers. The bus moved on in this fashion to Marseille, passengers getting off and getting on, and the overburdened vehicle sagging as it moved along the road.

Finally—and perhaps somewhat miraculously—the bus arrived safely at its destination. Virginia concluded that "you can well imagine how this state of things paralyzes the life of the country and how anyone who has the slightest excuse will gladly postpone even an important trip." But in Virginia's real work as an intelligence agent, postponing important trips could mean the difference between life and death, so she did everything she could to complete her missions as quickly as possible.

CHAPTER 9

TAKING CARE OF BRITISH AGENTS

y October 1941, Virginia was based in Lyon, which was a better operational base for her than the city of Vichy. At the time, Lyon was the third-largest city in France, and the center of the Resistance. Virginia said, "I can go and see things from there. Travel being slightly less horrible than from Vichy."

Virginia also noted that she had made valuable contacts in assessing the situation for British intelligence, and she had ". . . made such a lot of friends, doctors, business men, a few newspaper people (they are so daft I don't like them though), refugees, professors." At this time, the United States had still not entered the war and Virginia developed a close working relationship with George Whittinghill, the US vice consul in Lyon who represented British interests as well.

Because of Virginia's disability, some of her Resistance comrades referred to her as *la dame qui boite*, or the "limping lady." She took to referring to her artificial limb as Cuthbert. Virginia had befriended a redheaded doctor who liked to go hunting, and her hunting accident from years before wasn't far from her mind when Virginia noted that "I'm going shooting again—I shall keep Cuthbert well out of the way."

Several days after New Year's Day 1942, Virginia was propped up in her Lyon hotel bed with a typewriter balanced on her knee, writing to a friend. "All things in series of three, as usual," she typed. "A cold in the head, an ache in the thorax and mingled snow, rain and slush out of doors . . . The dark days are fairly abysmal and a short English word describes one's mood. The word, you know, is written - h- -, purest Anglo-Saxon!"

Virginia went on to relate to her friend that letters from America had virtually ceased since December, when the United States formally entered the war against both Japan and Germany. She was still waiting to receive a fruitcake her mother had sent from Maryland. Virginia's letter was lighthearted in tone but conveyed the many frustrations she, and so many others in wartime France, had to endure.

While she could pause to take a reflective look at her situation, the press of her duties was relentless. And other intelligence agents depended on her.

Back in December 1941, Lieutenant Peter Churchill, a young British Army officer of the Intelligence Corps, met with Maurice Buckmaster, the head of the SOE's France Section, in his London office. Several months prior, in September, Major Maurice Buckmaster became head of F Section, a position he held for the duration of the war. He had been a member of the SOE since March 1941, first as Information Officer, and then as the acting head of the SOE's Belgium Section. Buckmaster recalled that he was "eager to serve Britain by helping France."

Buckmaster had been a brilliant student, studying at Oxford University. He would later go to Paris and work for the French newspaper *Le Matin*, and subsequently at Ford Motor in France and then Great Britain. With the war approaching, Buckmaster joined the British military, saw combat, and ultimately joined the SOE. The demands of his job were intense: "We worked eighteen hours a day. We slept whenever we could—if we couldn't, we went without sleep altogether. Our life was totally devoted to SOE."

Maurice Buckmaster, head of the SOE's French Section.

Buckmaster, along with his staff, including his personal assistant, "the indispensable Vera Atkins," managed operations in France. Atkins was known for being helpful to agents in the field.

Lieutenant Churchill was reviewing his forthcoming trip where he would clandestinely infiltrate unoccupied France by submarine. After stressing to young Churchill that no one would think less of him if he decided not to undertake the mission, Buckmaster warned the lieutenant that ". . . if you should get caught, there is very little we can do for you." Churchill willingly accepted the risk to take on the mission.

Dressed as a French civilian, Churchill, who spoke French like a native, was to smuggle 2 million French francs to distribute to SOE agents in southern France in support of their operations. Half the money—1 million francs—was to be used to bribe officials to get ten members of the Resistance out of the Fort St. Nicholas prison in Marseille. Among the SOE agents he was supposed to meet in France was Virginia Hall.

One evening in early January 1942, the British submarine *P36* came within eight hundred yards of the Mediterranean shore of the French city Cannes. Peter paddled to land in the darkness in a canoe. Once ashore, he made his way through the cold winter weather to an old friend for food, sleep, and a change into dry clothes. He then took a bus to Antibes to meet his first contact. While the agent was away, Peter met with a physician who worked closely with the agent. The physician informed Peter that the local Resistance organization was in serious need of a skilled shortwave radio operator to communicate with London. They also needed additional funds in order to continue to function.

Peter could not help with the radio operator, but he could make a generous donation to the local Resistance effort from the money belt he was concealing under his clothes. He gave the doctor 450,000 francs and asked him to send the following telegram to an address in England: "Annabelle quite recovered and sends love and kisses." When that message was received, SOE leaders would know that this part of the mission was successfully accomplished.

The next leg of Peter's journey took him to Lyon. Walking from the local train station, he passed the Hôtel Carlton, the Gestapo's headquarters in the city, which was guarded by several Vichy policemen. (The Gestapo was Nazi Germany's secret police organization, noted for its ruthlessness.) Peter walked into the lobby of the nearby Grand Nouvel Hotel and inquired at the reception desk for Mademoiselle Le Contre, the name Virginia used in Lyon at that time.

"Mademoiselle is not in, Monsieur," replied the receptionist. "She is usually out all day, and returns at about six o'clock in the evening." Peter said he would come back later that night. Hungry and tired, Peter spent the rest of the day looking forward to his meeting with Virginia. He mused:

> All I knew about Brigitte Le Contre was that she was a tall American girl of about thirty-three, whose occupation was that of a newspaper correspondent. At the War Office they did not seem to know whether she was a blonde or a brunette. However, they did know that she had one brass foot owing to some hunting accident, but this fact was said to be well concealed and to handicap her walking so little that her infirmity was neither a hindrance to herself nor a help to anyone trying to find her, unless that person went to the lengths of stamping on the feet of every girl in town who seemed to be around thirty years of age.

Later that evening, Virginia telephoned Churchill at his hotel and suggested they have dinner. They met in the lobby of Virginia's hotel, where, after a quick greeting, she ushered him out into the snow and to a small restaurant run by a Greek gentleman who greeted Virginia "like a loving daughter." She explained to her fellow SOE agent the realities of food rationing and the use of food tickets in Vichy France. Since the color of food tickets changed every year, among Churchill's tasks on this mission was to bring back to London copies of the latest food tickets in France so they could be successfully counterfeited.

Peter Churchill at the Hotel de la Postes in Saint-Jorioz, France.

The proprietor came out and provided Virginia and Peter two large menus with a wide variety of selections. Peter was astonished at the choices while there was such a severe food shortage—with much of France's produce being confiscated by the Nazis for consumption in Germany. Virginia explained that "Lyon is better provided than most places. But you can't eat like this anywhere. This is a black-market restaurant."

"Isn't he taking a risk?" Peter asked, regarding the proprietor.

"No," replied Virginia. "He bribes the right people."

As the dinner progressed, Virginia told Peter that she would arrange for him to meet another agent named Charles. She then leaned over the table toward him and said, "By the way, I'm not an inquisitive person, but it's my turn to ask questions now. Your French is so perfect that I take it you are French."

Peter was flattered at the compliment of his language skills, but he felt no need to share anything more of his background than necessary. Instead, he proceeded to provide Virginia with his cover story. If she was ever asked to explain her relationship with him, she should state that his name was Pierre Chauvet, and "that I was a French Liaison Officer with the 50th Division [who] escaped capture at St. Valéry and made his way to Corsica." He noted that the War Office had even gone to the trouble of contacting one of Peter's friends in Corsica who would back up the story if any inquiries were ever made. He emphasized to Virginia, "as far as you're concerned, I've only just come over via Marseille and, because I was running short of money I'm approaching you—who are a newspaper reporter—with a view to cadging a little free-lance work."

Virginia was impressed. "Well, that's one of the best cover stories I ever heard. Short, sweet, and to the point. As far as I can see, it also holds water in every respect. They must have got somebody with a real brain back home."

"You know how it is," Peter replied, "they simply love playing these games in England."

Virginia was quick to admonish her dinner companion. "We never name that place when we wish to speak of it. Instead we say chez nous—at home. The other word is apt to attract attention." Even suggesting a tie to England could put both of them in serious jeopardy with the authorities. Peter vowed to remember that in the future.

The next day, Virginia met Peter in a local café. They were soon joined by another SOE agent, Charles, a tall, slim young man who had arrived in the area six months before. Virginia left the two men to talk while she attended to other business. Charles lived on the outskirts of Lyon in a modest house, carrying out his activities without attracting attention from the local authorities. To sustain the local group's operations, Peter provided Charles with 250,000 francs.

Peter gave Charles two tasks. First, to not only provide Peter with ration cards, but also a sample of every ration card issued

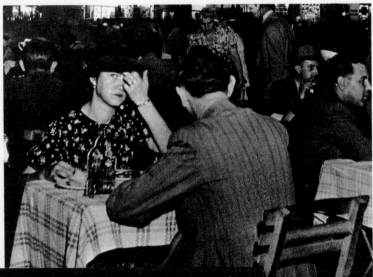

At an open-air café in Marseille, a woman pretends to adjust her hair while actually signaling to her friend the forbidden "V for Victory" sign.

in France. Second, Peter wanted him to identify half a dozen or so sites in the countryside north of Lyon that would be desirable for parachute and airplane landings. Specifically, they were looking for places close to the banks of two rivers in the area, since pilots could more easily see ground next to the rivers in the moonlight. The two men discussed the process of making contact with airplanes with equipment from the ground and how to provide signals and illuminate the landing area for drops and plane landings.

Later, Charles slid a folded newspaper across the table to Peter. He suggested Peter excuse himself from the table and, to shield himself from prying eyes, go to the toilet to examine the newspaper's contents. When he did so, Peter was delighted to see that it contained the sample ration books and other information he was looking for. Peter then placed a piece of paper into the newspaper that had the address of a town in England along with the message: "Leonore now flourishing." It would inform SOE headquarters that Peter had successfully completed another part of his mission. He returned to the table, handed the newspaper back to Charles, and asked that Virginia send the telegram message as soon as possible.

Then Peter took the train from Lyon to Marseille to make his next contact, a young man with the code name Olivier. He was grateful that Virginia had gone to Marseille in advance to facilitate the meeting. As the train raced through the winter cold toward Marseille, Peter reflected about Virginia. "She had struck me as a woman who would overcome any obstacle, and if I was inclined to shudder at her accent, I thought it was perhaps preferable that it was so obvious, otherwise it might have aroused suspicions through a state of near perfection."

When Peter's train pulled up to the station in Marseille, Virginia was on the platform waiting for him. Marseille was a port city of great strategic value. Because of this, there was a significant Gestapo presence in the area, making it a particularly challenging operational environment for the Resistance.

Virginia skillfully maneuvered Peter past a potential security obstacle and out of the train station onto the streets of Marseille. They walked past the Hôtel Splendide, which Virginia pointed out as being Gestapo headquarters. There was no snow on the ground in the city, but it was freezing. The streets were thronged with people, many of whom looked thin, hungry, and poor. As the two agents walked along, Peter was impressed with the speed and ease with which Virginia walked along the crowded pavements. He couldn't resist asking about her leg.

"Is it true about your foot, Germaine?" he asked, referring to Virginia by her alias.

"Yes," she replied with a smile. "It's actually made of aluminum and there's an opening where it fits round the heel."

"Good heavens!" Peter replied. "A walking ground-floor letter box that nobody would ever find. Hermes had nothing on you, Germaine."

"You're right. You'd be surprised at what goes into my aluminum puppy."

Virginia introduced Peter to Olivier, the SOE's representative in

Marseille: "a fair-haired youth whose clothes and manner were sober." Olivier set Peter up in a dingy room in a small hotel and gave him directions to where he would have to meet someone the next morning. Peter did not share with Virginia or Olivier the reason for his meeting the following day. To the extent possible, London tried to keep agents' missions and information compartmented to protect secrecy and the security of the agents.

The next morning, Peter met with the manager of a large ice factory in Marseille, requesting his assistance in freeing the ten men from prison and offering money to help him accomplish that goal. The man heard Peter out but ultimately declined to help. He told Peter, "I sympathize with their lot and your anxiety to get them out, but I cannot afford to associate myself with such a deal, as I am too well known in Marseille, and the news would get around at once if I touched it." The man did say, however, that he would try to help one of the men, who was formerly a junior officer on his staff.

Discouraged and disgusted at his inability to enlist the factory manager in his effort to free the men, Peter found the café where Virginia said she would meet him and sat down opposite her at a table. She was writing postcards and, looking at the expression on his face, she said, "What's eating you?" She went on to inquire, "Why don't you tell me what's happened, or is it a state secret?"

"I suppose they intended it to be in London. Personally, I'd hoped to bring it off on my own, too. But since you're on the spot, two heads are sure to be better than one."

"I'm all ears," said Virginia.

"I was supposed to get a local man to help in springing ten men out of prison, but he won't play."

"Is *that* all?"

"Isn't it enough?"

"Depends."

"On what?" asked Peter.

"The size of the bribe."

"Anything up to a million," Peter replied. That was almost all he had in the budget London had given him for this purpose.

"Child's play," Virginia said teasingly. "What do they think we do out here? Consort with princes and high society? Why, there isn't one of us who hasn't got at least a couple of unscrupulous lawyers up his sleeve who would jump at a crooked assignment like that. If these prisoners are held in Marseille, Olivier will handle it for you. He's an expert at such transactions, and I'm a little too busy on a similar proposition in Lyon to take it on just now."

Olivier soon joined them in the café and readily agreed to take on the assignment. He was somewhat incredulous that Peter hadn't told him about it in the first place. All Olivier said of the matter was "If only you'd told me about this before, I could have spared you this morning's goose chase."

Now the only thing left for Peter to do on this matter was to pass the money to Olivier. The two men excused themselves and went to the café's toilet, and locked themselves in. When they rejoined Virginia at the table, Peter had one million fewer francs in his money belt, and Olivier had suddenly become a millionaire. Peter discreetly handed Virginia a note with an address to another British town and the following message: "Marius' first tooth only visible as yet." He asked Virginia to send it at her earliest convenience. It would inform London that Peter had now completed his mission in France.

With his mission done, Peter needed to get back to London. He had hoped to bribe black market sources to get there by sea, but that soon proved not to be a possibility. Peter resigned himself to crossing the Pyrénées Mountains on foot into Spain. On his way to a rendezvous with Virginia to discuss those arrangements, he cut through a small side street. He soon found his way blocked by two Vichy security officials. With most of his money gone, Peter felt somewhat confident that he could bluff his way out of the situation.

"Your identity card!" demanded one of the men. Peter produced his wallet and took out his card.

"Nice lot of bank notes tucked away in that wallet," said the man.

"What about them?" Peter replied. He then noticed the other man stiffened somewhat and pushed something forward in his overcoat pocket. Peter wondered if it could be a gun.

"We're looking for likely people to volunteer for work in Germany, but I think we could come to terms. After all, one must live and let live, Monsieur."

"How much do you want?" Peter asked.

"Let's see," said the man, scrutinizing Peter's identity card. "Age: twenty-nine. Profession: Free-lance journalist. Not exactly a reserved occupation for a healthy young man, is it? If we were to take you along to headquarters you wouldn't get very far on that. I think, on the whole, if you were to empty that bulging compartment we might call it a deal."

"But that's all I've got in the world," Peter implored.

"Monsieur, you still have your freedom," said the man as he pocketed the wallet's contents.

"Charming!" Peter replied as he went on his way. The two Vichy officials got all they wanted from the exchange. While Peter had lost twenty-five thousand francs, he still had sixty-five thousand francs hidden in his money belt, which he would need to get out of France. He was both angry at having been robbed and relieved that the confrontation was over. It could have gone much worse.

Peter ultimately made his way back to England. But Virginia had been indispensable to his mission's success.

Another SOE agent Virginia assisted was Denis Rake, who was born in Belgium and came to Great Britain after World War I. He was an actor, appearing in musical comedies such as *No, No, Nanette*. At the outset of hostilities, he joined the British Army. Wanting to test his abilities and make a difference, Denis ultimately found his way into the SOE and trained to be a wireless telegraph operator. That, along with his fluency in French, made him particularly valuable to British intelligence. He was given the code name Alain.

Denis was placed on a camouflaged fishing boat headed for Gibraltar and, ultimately, southern France. His cover story was that of a Belgian businessman who was trying to obtain business contracts in France. From Gibraltar, Denis transferred to another boat under a Portuguese flag, and two nights later, a small boat dropped him on the beach near Juan-les-Pins, a resort town in southeastern France on the Côte d'Azur.

He landed in France carrying one suitcase with his wireless set and the other containing his personal belongings along with a great deal of money to fund his operations. The money had been intentionally "dirtied" by spattering the notes with oil and grease, marking them up, bending their edges, and crumpling them to keep them from looking like new bank notes, which usually created suspicion during a time of scarcity.

Eventually, Denis and an SOE colleague named Clément took the train to Lyon to begin their mission. At a small café on the Quai Perrache, they met their SOE contact, Virginia—"a tall, fair-haired woman of striking handsomeness" who was known to them as Renée. Denis was put up in a small, shabby hotel close to a railway bridge. That first night in Lyon, Denis and Clément went to see a film. For Denis, it was the first opportunity to relax since he had come to France as an agent. As the lights came up in the theater at the film's conclusion, Denis exclaimed to his colleague in English: "How marvelous this is!" Realizing the major security compromise, the two quickly left the theater.

Virginia tapped into her local contacts and arranged for Denis to operate his wireless telegraph at a number of safe houses in Lyon. After almost a month, the surly hotel manager informed Denis that his room in the nearly vacant establishment was needed and he had to look for lodgings elsewhere immediately. Denis went to Virginia for help.

"We should have found you somewhere else before," she told him. "I don't much like the idea of you living in a hotel anyway."

Clément suggested telling the hotel manager the truth about Denis. "He'll probably change his tune if we tell him you're a British officer."

Virginia was incredulous. "Shut up," she replied. "That's just about the most stupid idea I've ever heard."

The next day, Virginia met with Denis in the Place Lyautey. Denis had become increasingly anxious about his living situation as he had observed the hotel manager walking with a member of the Milice, the French militia who fought against the Resistance. Denis quickly paid his bill and checked out of the hotel. Virginia had provided an identity card and a work card, which gave Denis a cover as a worker for France's state-owned railway.

"I must have somewhere for tonight," he told Virginia.

"It's all right," she replied. "I've fixed something for you. It isn't very grand, I'm afraid."

Virginia took Denis to rooms in an attic in the Rue Violette la Chatte, where they were greeted by "a hard looking woman with a cigarette stuck between red-purple lips."

The prostitute asked Virginia, "What's it all about, love?"

"I want a room for my friend," Virginia replied. "Guillaume told you, didn't he?"

"Well, I see," she said. "Means I've got to move."

"Yes, of course, we'll compensate you whatever you think is fair. My friend wants to move in today."

"You're in a hurry, love, aren't you?"

The prostitute was inquisitive, wondering about Denis's true identity and the nature of Virginia's interest in him. Was he an escaped prisoner? The prostitute explained that she "loved soldiers" and would have to constrain herself from comforting Denis herself. Ultimately, Virginia deflected her questions and negotiated satisfactory terms so Denis could move into the prostitute's perfume-laden apartment. Once again, Virginia cleared the way for another agent to continue their work for the Resistance.

Eventually, the Milice began asking questions about Clément, and Virginia moved quickly to find new quarters for Clément and Denis. After receiving instructions from London, Clément fled France, arriving in England through Spain. Because Denis's wireless skills were so valuable, Virginia helped him relocate to Paris, where he worked with another Resistance group.

At great risk to herself, Virginia helped a large number of people, including fellow agents, Resistance members, downed Allied pilots, and escaped prisoners of war. But as hard as Virginia worked to aid her fellow agents, she would sometimes feel frustrated, if not exasperated, that SOE headquarters in London wasn't doing more to effectively support operations in France.

For example, two of Virginia's fellow agents had parachuted into the fields of the Sarthe Department of northwest France in late January of 1942. The pilot dropped them over eighteen miles off course from their intended destination, with one agent narrowly avoiding being impaled on stakes in a vineyard. Because they landed off target, there was no reception committee for the two men except for a dog at the farm where they landed.

The agents buried their gear and walked to Tours, then traveled to Paris, before finally arriving in Marseille, where Virginia picked them up and brought them back to Lyon. Once there, she sent the two men to a colleague in the South of France who needed extra assistance.

Virginia complained to London that the agents apparently weren't given information about who they were to contact in France. The situation was frustrating "because a month of aimless and seemingly hopeless wandering, without reliable means of obtaining food tickets, etc., has been discouraging, especially after having been landed in the wrong place and almost been split upon a stake." Unable to conceal her disappointment, she added, "It isn't really good enough." Virginia also called on London to provide a "good executive and organizer."

"There are a lot of contacts," she noted, "but they need following up and organizing, none of which has been done, to my knowledge."

In a communication to London in early March 1942, Virginia mentioned that nine Free French officers had landed in France in the previous several weeks. She was troubled that she was not being given more information about such matters so she could provide assistance and avoid mishaps. "It would be greatly appreciated if we could be informed of the identity of such men and when they land, to avoid any tragic mistakes and so that I could warn my French contacts, or confirm, as the case might be." Making headquarters aware of the operational challenges on the ground would be an ongoing struggle for Virginia and other SOE agents.

ABBÉ ALESCH: FRIEND OR FOE?

*U*p to the end of July 1942, Virginia continued to receive War Office Liaison (W.O.L.) information through Dr. Jean Rousset. But Dr. Rousset said that because of the difficulty in making the weekly trip to visit her, Virginia would be seeing a courier instead. He told her that she "could have complete confidence in the courier and give him both the rest of the money [she] had for him (150 grand) and a couple of documents [she] had promised him . . ."

The courier left his package with Dr. Rousset, but because Virginia had not deposited her package for the courier, and the courier was in a hurry, he returned to Paris stating that he'd come back within a week. The courier did so on August 25, 1942, and he was insistent on seeing Virginia. As soon as Dr. Rousset advised

Virginia that the courier had arrived, Virginia took the money and went to see him.

Virginia met the courier in one of Dr. Rousset's waiting rooms. Standing before her was a man about five feet, two inches tall, of normal build, bald but with light brown hair around the edges, prominent cheekbones, penetrating light blue eyes, thin lips, and a cleft chin. He introduced himself to Virginia as Abbé Alesch. (An *abbé* in France is a lower-ranking clergyman.) He told Virginia that he was using the name of D'Acquin—after St. Thomas Aquinas—and gave the name of his hotel next to the cathedral in Lyon, as well as his address in a suburb of Paris.

A British agent from Paris had been providing Virginia with reports that she had been asked to pass along to London. However, Alesch told Virginia that agent had disappeared and the circuit was disorganized. What should he do? The *abbé* also warned Virginia that the zone she was living in was dangerous and that "great prudence should be observed." In reply, Virginia told him to return to Paris and to do what he could to put those at risk into safety. In ten days, Virginia would have instructions for him.

The *abbé* spoke French with "a pronounced German accent," which troubled Virginia. She was wary of him. He later told her that he was Alsatian—one of the German-speaking inhabitants of the French region of Alsace—which Virginia thought explained his accent. Still, could he be working for the Germans? Virginia recalled: "He did not make a very favorable impression on me and I wired to London giving his name and address, asking that he be checked by S.I.S. [Great Britain's Secret Intelligence Service] agents in Paris and that I be given instructions as to what to do with him."

London responded to Virginia's query by directing her to "continue to take his stuff, to have him reorganized and to give him one hundred thousand francs and films for microphoto work." Virginia saw the *abbé* again in September 1942, at which time she gave him the money, his instructions, and the films. It was the last time the two would meet.

At that meeting, Alesch reported to Virginia that several of their agents had been arrested or unaccountably vanished. Virginia noted that

> he also says that he is out adrift now . . . He asked instructions and advice and insisted that he be put in touch with someone else as well as myself, in case I disappeared over night. In short he was a problem child. I told him to go back to Paris to try to trace the people thru [*sic*] the person who distributes the money . . . to try to reorganize and then to return here about the twentieth of September to report and receive his instructions.

Because Virginia was wary of Alesch, she would not give him her true name or tell him where she lived. After the September meeting, Virginia refused to meet with the *abbé* again, and he was directed to simply place his information in the designated letter box. Dr. Rousset, who Virginia considered a good Catholic, continued to insist that her doubts about the *abbé* were unfounded, as Alesch had the manners of an *abbé*.

It would later turn out that Virginia's concerns were justified.

CHAPTER 11

THE RIVER IS RISING: VIRGINIA'S FINAL DAYS IN LYON

*O*ne day in September 1942, Virginia checked her letter box in Lyon and found an unsigned note indicating that Alex, a Resistance member, and two of his colleagues, Fabian and Justin, had been arrested. Virginia immediately went to the local prison to make inquiries, but the guard at the gate denied knowing anything about the matter.

A contact Virginia referred to as Pompey confirmed that the men were in prison and he promised to learn what the charges were against them. Virginia noted, however, that Pompey "wasn't very active so far as help was concerned, nor did he tell me how or why they were arrested."

Virginia was ultimately able to determine what happened to the men. A nervous Justin was left alone in a café and instantly drew the attention of a police inspector, who asked what his business was in the area. The inspector was not satisfied with the answers and searched the contents of Justin's pockets. The money he was carrying looked suspiciously new, and the inspector assumed that Justin was an agent who had come from England or Germany. When Justin's two companions stopped by, the inspector detained them as well and took all three men to the police station.

Adding to the police's suspicions, Fabian and Alex had identity cards from different towns but made out in the same handwriting. Still, there were individuals sympathetic to the Resistance at the police station who allowed the men to burn a few of their notes and papers, as well as conceal some of their other incriminating possessions. As Virginia noted, "the result is that all three were held but that there was no serious charge against them."

Alex and Fabian were ultimately sent to Castres, in southern France, and Justin was placed in a camp not far from Toulouse. Virginia supported them making an escape attempt by providing the men with instructions and money. However, Pompey got wind of the proposed escape and asked that the attempt be delayed by several weeks. Virginia complied with his request. After two weeks of captivity, the effort to release them finally went forward. She expressed concern, however, that the two men in Castres would be sent to separate camps, which would make their escape more complicated.

Two sympathetic French policemen came to see Virginia, who informed her that they would engineer an escape for Alex and his companions in early October. One would be placed in the country and the other two would enter a clinic while they awaited a small boat or some other means of escape. Virginia promised one of the security men that if he was able to successfully arrange this escape, she would help him get to England. Virginia also agreed to Pompey's request to send the men out of France after their escape.

In addition, Pompey was insistent that Virginia help a young friend of his to leave France and escape into Spain. Pompey told Virginia that the young man was going on a mission to Spain and would return to France. Virginia, however, suspected that the young man, married to an Englishwoman and the father of two young boys, actually wanted to travel on to England. In addition, the young man only spoke English and French. Despite Virginia's mistrust of Pompey, she stated that "I felt that I had to throw a bone to the lion." She made the travel arrangements as a favor to Pompey. But she asked London to inform her if the man did, in fact, arrive there. "Let me know, because it is always nice to know how much people are lying to one."

It's unclear what became of these individuals. But that was often the case dealing with escapees. One did one's best for them and hoped things would ultimately work out.

In the first week of October, Virginia stated that she was moving to an apartment on the sixth floor of a building. The building didn't have an elevator, undoubtedly making it somewhat challenging for Virginia, who had to make the climb with her artificial leg. She complained that "somebody has been a dope and given my name and address away and I am getting astounding personages here who want to go to England."

Not only did Virginia not know some of the people coming to her home, she did not know the people who referred them to her. But she was determined to do whatever she could for people in need. One of the British agents Virginia assisted observed, "If you sit in her kitchen long enough, you will see most people pass through with one sort of trouble or other, which she promptly deals with."

While generally cautious, Virginia's willingness to perform her mission sometimes led others to question her operational security. For example, one British agent visited her apartment at a time when it was a major rendezvous for SOE agents. He "found the entire passage-way absolutely dripping with aerial [radio antenna], well over 70 ft. of it. It was such a blatant announcement of the agent's activities" that the agent "left immediately and never returned."

Virginia was aware that her address in Lyon had been provided to the pro-Nazi Vichy authorities. While her name had not been provided to them, she realized that "it wouldn't be hard to guess." Her personal security was increasingly at risk. As the Gestapo became aware of Virginia and her activities, they issued a frightening edict: "The woman who limps is one of the most dangerous Allied agents in France. We must find and destroy her."

Virginia knew her luck was running out, and she needed to do something about it. She wrote London: ". . . I think my time is about up and request that you arrange a Clipper [airplane] passage for me for the end of October—real or fake—to permit me to get in my visas and clear out if necessary." As a security precaution, she added that she was "trying to see no one at my flat for the time being."

Virginia informed London that a particular Resistance leader had left Lyon. He considered himself the head of Le Coq enchaîné, a French Resistance group in the Lyon area. But Virginia reported that the group "has practically blown up—one man was taken and gave away about twenty others. I don't know how or where it will end." Nevertheless, Virginia asked for more instructions related to arms and their distribution. Yet she offered a caution as well. She warned London that "if you go arming local organizations, as I have already pointed out, you are going to get a state of bloody anarchy here one day when you will need a little unity." Virginia was undoubtedly anticipating the dynamics in France when it would one day be liberated from the German occupation.

CHAPTER 12

VIRGINIA'S ESCAPE

*T*oward the end of 1942, it became clear that it was just a matter of time before unoccupied France would soon be overtaken by Germany. The threat to Virginia and her Resistance colleagues was growing.

On November 5, 1942, Maurice Buckmaster followed up with arrangements for Virginia's departure, emphasizing that George Backer of the *New York Post* was recalling her from France. He also provided details regarding Virginia's passport as a pre-condition before she could be provided transport facilities in Lisbon, Portugal. Buckmaster requested that the *New York Post*'s home office book passage for Virginia on a Clipper aircraft and asked that Virginia be informed directly about this by Backer or through the US Consulate in Lyon.

On Saturday, November 7, 1942, Philomène, as Virginia was then known, was informed by the American Consulate that an invasion of North Africa was imminent, and that she should seriously consider leaving Lyon as soon as possible unless she wished to "stay in forced residence for the duration" of hostilities. While Virginia was a risk taker, she was also sensible, and she started preparing for her departure. She immediately began to destroy all records at her home and at work. She gave the seals, blank documents, and money she had on hand—approximately 200,000 francs—to a colleague, asking him to look after her other contacts in the French Resistance. Virginia also told her colleagues that if a German occupation of Vichy France were to take place, "they should not be surprised by my abrupt departure."

Lyon was becoming a less hospitable operational base for Virginia, and it was clear her days there were numbered. In November 1942, Klaus Barbie was made head of the Gestapo in Lyon, where he established his headquarters in the Hôtel Terminus. He would become known as "the Butcher of Lyon" for his brutality in torturing and executing

Klaus Barbie.

prisoners. Barbie had apparently heard of Virginia's activities in support of the Resistance. An agent reported that Barbie, mistaking Virginia's country of origin, stated that "he would give anything to put his hands on that Canadian bitch."

On Sunday morning, November 8, 1942, Virginia learned about Operation Torch, the American and British invasion of French North Africa, which was launched that day. The Germans were now certain to finally take over unoccupied France. Security procedures in the free zone of France were somewhat lax and that was certain to change when the Germans invaded the region. (The Germans would invade southern France on November 11.)

Virginia was strongly encouraged to leave France immediately. She tried to reach out to two of her contacts, but neither showed up to meet with her. "I decided that they were nervous about coming to the flat or else took it for granted that I had left."

At 9:00 that evening, one of Virginia's contacts told her that the Germans were expected to arrive in Lyon sometime between midnight and Monday morning. She knew she had to leave immediately.

She could be proud of what she had accomplished during her operational tour of France. As one scholar of the SOE put it, Virginia had "an imperturbable temper; she took risks often but intelligently, and [. . .] was never once arrested nor more than superficially questioned." Indeed, "without her indispensable work about half of F section's early operations in France could never have been carried out at all."

Virginia packed her bag and took the 11:00 p.m. train from Lyon to Perpignan, a small city in southern France, close to the Mediterranean. When she arrived, Virginia approached a man, code-named Gilbert, who could usually be found on the city square between 2:00 p.m. and 3:00 p.m. every day. Gilbert obtained guides for Virginia, at a cost of 20,000 francs per person. Virginia paid for herself, as well as three other companions who had no money.

Virginia left Perpignan on the night of Wednesday, November 11, 1942, and traveled over the Pyrénées Mountains with a Spanish guide as well as "two London-based Frenchmen, and a Congo Captain from Belgium." They did not use the regular escape lines. The group traveled via Villefranche by foot to Lavelanet, a small French town in the Midi-Pyrénées. They hiked over the Col de Tivoli, and then down about ten miles from Camprodon, a town in Spain located in the Pyrénées near the border with France. From there, she and her companions reached the town of Sant Joan de les Abadesses in Catalonia, Spain.

The hike to freedom was a challenge, particularly for Virginia with her prosthetic leg. One of her radio transmissions to London reported that Virginia was having difficulty with her artificial limb. She stated, "Cuthbert is giving me trouble, but I can cope." The London operator, apparently unaware of Virginia's nickname for her prosthetic leg, replied, "If Cuthbert is giving you trouble, have him eliminated."

In the predawn hours of Saturday, November 14, Virginia and her group hoped to catch the 5:45 train there to Barcelona,

Allied troops on the beaches near Algiers, Algeria, for Operation Torch.

Spain. They didn't make it. When they arrived in the town at 4:30 a.m., they were picked up by local authorities because they didn't have any papers. Virginia was placed in a prison for prostitutes, and she tried to make the most of her three weeks in jail. During her daily half hour of activity in the prison yard, Virginia befriended an eighty-two-year-old woman who was also jailed there.

A younger woman Virginia befriended proved particularly useful. When this young prostitute was finally released, she took with her a letter from Virginia and mailed it to the US Consulate in Barcelona. Virginia would be released from jail on Wednesday evening, December 2, 1942, as a result of the efforts of the US Consulate. And on January 19, 1943, Virginia returned to the United Kingdom.

ON THE SIDELINES
IN SPAIN

*A*fter Virginia's narrow escape from Nazi-occupied France and her release from prison in Spain, she had the opportunity to rest and recover from her experience. She told her SOE colleagues about the situation in France and the details of her operational activities, as well as providing her best knowledge of the location of their agents' wireless telegraph sets.

Yet Virginia was not content to remain on the sidelines. She wanted to return to France, but her superiors in the SOE believed it was not safe for her to. Instead, she was offered the opportunity to work in Spain.

In early May 1943, Virginia and several of her SOE colleagues met to discuss her new assignment. Having obtained a transit visa for Portugal and another for Spain as her final destination, Virginia was to work in Spain where her cover was again to be that of a foreign correspondent; this time for the *Chicago Times* newspaper. In order to establish her credibility with the Spanish authorities, her superiors instructed Virginia to take two to three months and work exclusively as a correspondent before beginning her clandestine SOE work.

In discussing her intelligence work—which included identifying "safe houses and possible personnel for future recruitment"—Virginia raised the question of how she should interact with the American community in Spain. Her British colleagues made it clear to Virginia that "while she should in no way cold-shoulder them, they should not be given any opportunity of suspecting that she was working for the SOE, as no intercommunication was desirable between American and British representatives in the field." Protecting her operational cover was a high priority.

SOE officials realized that they were fortunate to have an agent of Virginia's caliber working there. As one official told another: "I think you will find her both intelligent, useful and pleasant to work with. She certainly is capable of getting things done . . ." The bureaucratic transition became formalized on May 5, 1943, when the SOE asked for approval for Virginia to transfer from F Section to work in Spain, and that the payroll would reflect that fact effective June 1, 1943. Arrangements were also made for Virginia "to travel by the first plane available" to Spain after May 15, 1943. Soon, Virginia was in Madrid.

There was some concern about paying Virginia adequately for her mission in Spain. She had no embassy affiliation, and while her cover was as a journalist, unfortunately "her American editors will pay almost nothing for articles on Spain." Yet Virginia needed to be able to have an adequate social profile to perform her mission, "since much of her usefulness will depend on her being able to give and accept entertainment . . ."

Virginia's fame within the tight world of the British government's clandestine security service had grown, and she received notable recognition for her earlier service in France. Her file in the British Archive contains the following testimonial dated October 19, 1942:

> Since August 1941, when this lady went into the field on our behalf, she has devoted herself whole-heartedly to our work without regard to the dangerous position in which her activities would place her if they were realized by the Vichy authorities. She has been indefatigable in her constant support and assistance for our agents, combining a high degree of organizing ability with a clear-sighted appreciation of our needs. She has become a vital link between ourselves and various operational groups in the field, and her services for us cannot be too highly praised.

In a telegram to Madrid on July 18, 1943, Virginia was informed, and congratulated by her colleagues, that the United Kingdom was making her a Member of the Order of the British Empire (MBE) for her outstanding achievement. However, "in view of her nationality and cover, essential celebrations remain strictly private." This was fine with Virginia as she wished to continue serving as an intelligence agent and needed to maintain her undercover status.

Whatever gratification Virginia received from being awarded the MBE, it didn't compensate for what she considered the futility of the work she was undertaking in Spain. In her desire to be useful, Virginia read the French and German newspapers daily. She offered to clip and share newspaper articles of interest with her SOE colleagues. But such activities, while marginally helpful, weren't enough to make Virginia feel as if she was making a meaningful contribution to the war effort.

In early October, Virginia notified Maurice Buckmaster and his colleagues in London that she wished to leave Spain and return to France. She felt that she was sidelined in the war effort and wanted to be involved. "I've given this a good four months try and come to the conclusion that it really is a waste of time and money." Virginia had met up with "two of my very own boys here"—agents with whom she'd already worked in France—and proposed returning with them as a radio operator. "I can learn the radio quickly enough in spite of skepticism in some quarters," she added. Virginia then made her most heartfelt appeal to Buckmaster:

When I came out here I thought that I would be able to help F. Section people, but I don't and can't. I am not doing a job. I am simply living pleasantly and wasting time. It isn't worthwhile and after all, my neck is my own, and if I am willing to get a crick in it because there is a war on . . . Well, anyhow, I put it up to you. I think I can do a job for you along with my two boys. They think I can too and I trust that you will let us try, because we are all three very much in earnest about this bloody war.

Maurice Buckmaster responded to Virginia on October 6, 1943, in a letter affectionately addressed to "Dearest Doodles." "What a wonder you are!" he remarked. Buckmaster conceded that Virginia could learn radio "in no time" and that "the boys would love to have you in the field." But he also pointed out his view that the Gestapo would soon find out about Virginia's return to France, and that was why Buckmaster was refusing to send Virginia back. Buckmaster went on to state that:

You are really too well-known in the country and it would be wishful thinking believing that you could escape detection for more than a few days. You do realize, don't you, that what was previously a picnic, comparatively speaking, is now real war, and that the Gestapo are pulling in everything they can? You will object, I know, that it is your own neck—I agree, but we all know it is not only your own neck. It is the necks of all with whom you come into contact because the Boche [Germans] is good at patiently following trails, and sooner or later he will unravel the whole skein if he has a chance. We do not want to give him even half a chance by sending in anyone as remarkable as yourself at the moment.

Having closed the door on a return to France in the near term, Buckmaster put forward another proposal to Virginia. He told her, "If you are feeling that you are not pulling your weight where you are, why not come back to London and join us as a briefing officer for the boys?" Buckmaster wanted Virginia to return to F Section, where he told Virginia that her duties to her colleagues would require the following:

1) To meet them when they come back from the field, to hear what they have to say, to analyze it, and to see that they got their questions answered.
2) To see that they are properly looked after from the point of view of material things—i.e., clothes, equipment, etc. In other words, see that the clothing and equipment officers of F. Section produce the jobs in time and correctly.
3) To brief the new boys with the fruits of what you have yourself learned and what you have picked up from the latest arrivals.

Buckmaster conceded that these duties sounded like the same kind of "sit-down job" that Virginia was currently performing in Spain, but he said there was a possible advantage to it. The anticipated Allied D-Day invasion to liberate Europe would likely take place within the year, and when the SOE's officers went into the field in support of the invasion, Virginia would be well placed to join the effort. But Buckmaster wanted to be clear with Virginia on this point: "I obviously can make no promises as to this at the moment, but it is a possibility."

Soon, Virginia was informed that SOE management had approved of her returning to London to work, with her focusing on France. She was asked: "Will you, therefore, make the necessary plans to leave Spain in such a manner as will permit you to return there 'clean' at some future date should it be desirable for you to do so." Virginia returned to the United Kingdom from Madrid on November 29, 1943, and rejoined the SOE's French Section. She was one step closer to resuming the fight for France's liberation.

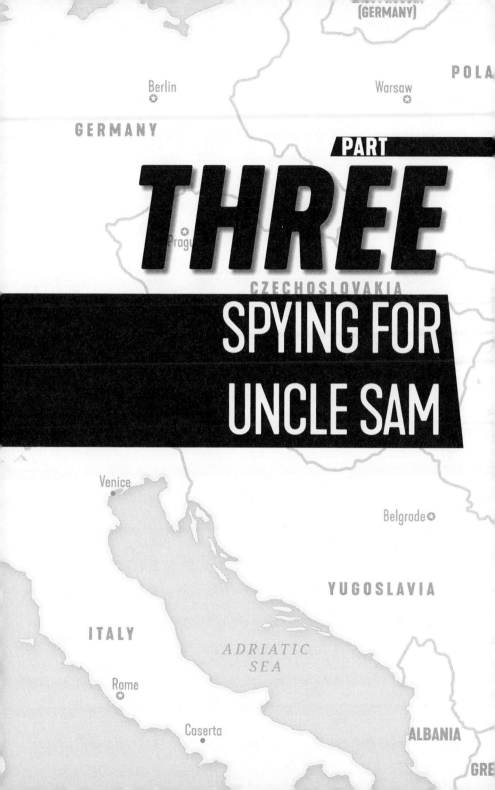

PART THREE

SPYING FOR UNCLE SAM

THE OSS: AMERICA'S WARTIME SPY SERVICE

In the years prior to World War II, the role of gathering information—in other words, intelligence—for the US government was largely left to the State Department and the armed services. Diplomats and military attachés posted overseas collected information in the course of their normal duties with foreign counterparts, and sometimes through secret contacts. Some of this information would make its way to senior policymakers in the administration, including the president. But there was no strategic approach to collecting and analyzing intelligence.

Robert Murphy, a senior diplomat, later recalled: "It must be confessed that our intelligence organization in 1940 was primitive and inadequate. It was timid, parochial, and operating strictly in the tradition of the Spanish-American War."

As another world war was approaching, President Franklin Roosevelt sought to bring a more strategic approach to intelligence. Roosevelt would ultimately turn to William Donovan to lead this effort.

William J. Donovan was a New York lawyer who had won the Medal of Honor in World War I for his heroism in combat and made a failed bid for governor of New York in 1932 as the Republican candidate. With war approaching, Donovan became a trusted advisor to President Roosevelt, who was impressed with Donovan's views on the important role of intelligence in modern warfare. In the summer of 1941, Roosevelt tapped Donovan to lead the effort to force the civilian and military services to cooperate more on intelligence matters. On July 11, 1941, President Roosevelt appointed Donovan as the Coordinator of Information (COI), a new civilian office attached to the White House, and placed him in charge of collecting and analyzing information related to national security. As the head of American intelligence during World War II, Donovan would return to active duty as a brigadier general and later was promoted to major general in November 1944.

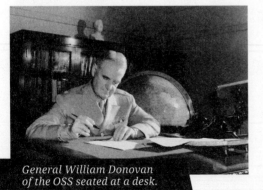

General William Donovan of the OSS seated at a desk.

On December 7, 1941, the Japanese launched a surprise attack on the US naval base at Pearl Harbor, Hawaii, leading America to declare war on Japan. Nazi Germany then declared war on the United States on December 11, 1941, and later that same day, the United States reciprocated and declared war on Germany. At the time that the United States formally entered World War II, Donovan's office had a staff of six hundred and a budget of $10 million, and was viewed suspiciously by the Federal Bureau of Investigation (FBI), the War Department's Military Intelligence Division (known as the G-2), and other agencies that considered the COI a competitor for their own intelligence roles and budgets.

The newly established Joint Chiefs of Staff (JCS) also became wary of Donovan's operation. The JCS became the president's military advisors, providing recommendations to the commander in chief on strategy and all aspects of war plans related to the navy and the army. The JCS allocated resources and "supervised the collection of strategic intelligence and the conduct of clandestine operations." It was decided to place Donovan's organization under the JCS, but in a way that preserved its autonomy and gave it access to the military's expanding resources. On June 13, 1942, Donovan's organization became the Office of Strategic Services (OSS). But this did not end bureaucratic turf battles that would persist throughout the war.

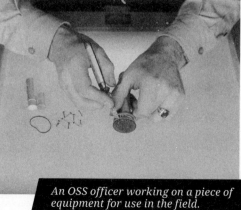

An OSS officer working on a piece of equipment for use in the field.

The OSS had a number of functions. Among the organization's elements, in addition to administrative and security support work, was a Research and

The inexpensive, OSS-designed, .45-caliber Liberator pistol was easy to use and widely distributed to partisan groups during the war.

Development Branch that was made up of technicians and engineers who developed spy gear and weapons. There was also a Research and Analysis Branch, which included scholars, diplomats, economists, historians, political scientists, psychologists, and others. Virginia would become a member of the OSS's Special Operations Branch (SO), the organization's component dedicated to running guerrilla campaigns, conducting sabotage, and generally subverting the enemy.

By late 1944, there were 13,000 men and women working for the OSS, many from the armed services. Approximately 7,500 of those employees served overseas, and about 4,500 OSS employees were women, with 900 of them serving abroad. In Fiscal Year 1945, the budget for the OSS was $43 million.

British and American intelligence were close partners during World War II, but it took time for this relationship to evolve. British officials had some concerns that the less experienced OSS might compromise British operations in occupied Europe, and Americans were concerned about their own operations being dependent on the intelligence service of another nation, no matter how friendly. But this bilateral intelligence relationship strengthened into a close and constructive working

In March 1945, OSS officer William E. Colby (standing) led a joint OSS-Norwegian special operations team into German-occupied Norway to conduct sabotage.

relationship as the two nations' common objectives and shared sacrifice dwarfed any differences.

The OSS Special Operations Branch, in particular, worked closely with Great Britain's SOE. The two organizations jointly created the "Jedburgh" teams to support the D-Day landings in the summer of 1944. Ultimately, there were ninety-three three-person Jedburgh teams consisting of two officers (usually an OSS officer and a British officer), along with a radio operator. Their mission was to assist the French Resistance and the advancing Allied forces, coordinating airdrops of supplies, and supporting sabotage and military attacks against German forces.

CHAPTER 15

THE GREAT ADVENTURE: VIRGINIA'S RETURN TO FRANCE

*P*hilippe de Vomécourt had worked with Virginia in Lyon—he knew her as Marie—and later took over the leadership of one of the groups she organized during her second tour of duty in wartime France. He recalled that "as a neutral she had done many things to help us. She had carried messages for us, she had gone where we could not go. She wheedled the police into releasing many prisoners, including escaping POWs and agents . . ."

But after her first operational tour of France with the SOE, Virginia decided she no longer wanted to be dependent on others to be a W/T operator. As she later said, "I became a radio operator because I had become distrustful of radio operators [who] were often careless. Also to be 'self contained'!" Virginia was determined, and in early 1944, she was trained to be a radio operator.

French Resistance fighters learning how to use a radio set.

When de Vomécourt met up with her later in the war, he said that Virginia recalled how she returned to France as a member of the OSS in 1944. According to de Vomécourt, Virginia explained to him what she had to do to return to France after she escaped through Spain and returned to England. He recounted their conversation:

"Your accent just isn't good enough," she was told—and by any normal standards they were absolutely right. But Virginia Hall was not to be measured by normal standards.

"You can't go back," they said.

"Why not?" she wanted to know.

"You'd be a danger—a danger to yourself, and a danger to your friends. You'd certainly be a danger to your radio operator."

"Well, suppose I learn how to work a radio—would you send me back then, on my own?"

"Oh yes," she was told, "all you've got to do is learn how to operate a radio and you can go back." And they laughed as they said it. They did not offer to teach her—and I cannot blame them for that.

But Virginia Hall ignored their laughs and paid for lessons in radio work with her own money. In three months she had learned how to receive and transmit messages. She went back to the powers that be at the SOE.

The OSS-trained communications officers at a facility in Prince William Forest Park, VA, before deploying them to the field.

"Now can I go back to France?" she asked. "I know how to work a radio—I don't need to take anyone with me." The promise had been given to her casually, thinking it an easy way to discourage her. But "Marie" was hard to discourage.

As March 1944 approached, Virginia was preparing herself to begin her second tour of France. This time, it would be far more dangerous as she was now known to the Nazis as an enemy intelligence agent.

Virginia's OSS companion for her return to France was an unlikely

Henry Laussucq: "Aramis."

intelligence officer. He was sixty-one years old, around five feet, nine inches tall with a heavy build. Born in Bordeaux, France, on December 24, 1882, his name was Henry Laurent Laussucq. His code name was Aramis, after one of the three musketeers from Alexandre Dumas's famous novel, and he was raised and educated in France. He had an engineering degree from the Sorbonne in Paris, as well as a degree from the École des Beaux-Arts in Paris.

Henry served in the French infantry during World War I, seeing combat against the Germans in St. Michel and the Argonne, receiving three wounds and five citations for bravery. In December 1929 he moved to New York City and became a US citizen. Henry worked as a freelance artist before serving at the *New York Journal-American* newspaper, where he worked as an art director, producing advertising layouts, illustrations, and promotions for eighty-five dollars per week.

Henry had tried to enlist in the US Army at the outset of World

War II, but he was denied because of his age. His oldest son, a French citizen, was a prisoner of war in Germany and another son was serving in the US Army Air Force. Henry wanted to join the fight against the Nazis as well. Applying for the OSS, Henry suggested that because of his training and experience, he might be useful as a mechanical or architectural draftsman, painter, or mapmaker. He was also fluent in French, with a slight knowledge of German, Spanish, and Italian. His interviewer noted that Henry was "in excellent physical form, despite age. Very energetic and good education—willing to undertake any mission." In August 1943, Henry joined the OSS.

Aramis was informed that his OSS mission was to travel to France and establish three hideouts, or safe houses, large enough to accommodate up to three individuals, and to be used as meeting places for members of the French Resistance. The first safe house was to be located in Paris; the second safe house was to be located approximately 62 miles southeast of Paris; and the third safe house was to be located approximately 124 miles southeast of the French capital. The circuit he was establishing was code-named Saint.

Aramis's guidance was straightforward. He should establish his headquarters in Paris, or as close to the capital as possible. It was suggested, quite unnecessarily, that he be careful, and that he be in Paris when the liberation of France occurred. All other potential initiatives were left to his discretion, but he was given one admonition by the OSS about protecting operations: "Do not

ARAMIS
1964

HECKLER   RG 226   E 92   Box 296   Fol. 184
WASH – REG – AD – 7

Drawing of Virginia Hall by Aramis.

get too thick with the French movements of the Resistance, their ideas on security being quite different from ours."

Virginia was going to accompany Aramis into France as his radio operator. She was getting her wish to return to France and continue fighting the Nazis. Virginia and Aramis had two meetings prior to their departure from England. Aramis was concerned, however, that Virginia was ordered to establish herself in the Creuse department in central France, some two hundred miles from Aramis in Paris, and therefore not easily accessible to him.

On March 19, their last day in London, Virginia and Aramis were greeted by Colonel Buckmaster and his assistant. Buckmaster liked to present his agents with a luxury item before they went off to the field. The colonel gave Aramis an alligator skin wallet, which Aramis suspected of having been made in Germany. Preparing to cross the English Channel, the two left London by train to the southern coast of England. They had a restful evening at the Redcliffe Hotel in Paignton, a seaside town on the coast of Tor Bay in Devon. The next day, which was sunny and balmy, American troops could be seen at the nearby seashore conducting military exercises.

On the evening of March 20, Virginia and Aramis were driven to a seaport some twenty to thirty miles away and placed aboard a small patrol vessel where the two changed into civilian clothes. The boat was piloted by Captain Peter Harratt.

They checked all their pockets to make sure there was no "pocket litter" (e.g., British hotel receipts, London subway tickets, non-French currency) that would undermine their new French cover identities. Then, as Aramis would later recall, "We came up on deck as the night was falling and the effect of the shimmering lights of what looked like a million crafts of all kinds was something unforgettable to behold. We had our meal at the officers table and pretty soon were on our way to the great adventure."

SETTING UP SHOP

*A*fter coming ashore on a French beach and beginning to hike inland, Virginia, Aramis, and the landing party reached the top of the cliff. Aramis, however, fell into a crevice and wrenched his knee, making it difficult for him to carry his heavy bag. The group continued their trek, crossing over hedges and barbed wire, before arriving at an abandoned cottage. They rested there and continued on to a farm where they were provided with food and drinks.

Next, they were driven by truck for several miles, and then they walked for another two miles. Aramis's swollen knee had become unbearable, and he could hardly stand up. Finally, they reached a farmhouse where they ate a meal. The village's veterinarian drove them to the medieval town of Morlaix, on Brittany's coast, to see a physician. *"Une entorse,"* the doctor pronounced after examining his patient. A sprain. The doctor bandaged the knee and informed Aramis that the injury would cause him pain for quite a while. Aramis would feel that pain for the rest of his time in France.

From the doctor's office, Virginia and Aramis walked to the railroad station, each carrying two bags. Around 7:00 that night, they boarded a train to Paris. While there were many German soldiers on the train, the older French gentleman and his "wife" attracted no attention. The train arrived in Paris at 6:30 the following morning. Virginia and Aramis passed unnoticed among the many other travelers carrying their own baggage. The two weary travelers took the Paris subway to the Invalides Metro station.

They met up with an old friend of Virginia's, Madame Long, who lived close to the Rue de Babylone, and found a room for Aramis in a nearby *pensione*, or boardinghouse. The landlady was a *Gaulliste*—a French citizen who rejected the Vichy collaboration with the Germans and supported General Charles de Gaulle in wanting to get France back in the war. Accordingly, the landlady did not require Aramis to fill out any registration form, making it a fairly safe place for him to stay. However, the boardinghouse was also inhabited by rowdy young people who constantly asked the increasingly uncomfortable Aramis to explain his frequent absences.

Virginia stayed in Madame Long's apartment. After further discussion with Aramis, however, Madame Long decided that he was excessively talkative and indiscreet. She informed Virginia that she didn't want Aramis coming by to visit her apartment. So Virginia thought it wise for her and Aramis to move on.

The following morning, Virginia stopped by Aramis's

boardinghouse and, apparently to spare him the true nature of Madame Long's concerns, told him that Madame Long was "very uneasy and fearful of her presence there."

The next day, Virginia and Aramis traveled to Creuse. Aramis purchased reserved seats on a train out of the Austerlitz station in Paris. They traveled to Saint-Sébastien, between Argenton and Limoges, arriving in the darkness at 6:30 a.m. With only a verbal description provided previously by an OSS colleague, the two trudged about three and a half miles through the French countryside to a farm at Maisons-sous-Crozant. Because of the pain in his knee, helping to carry the luggage was a particular ordeal for Aramis, and he kept up a steady stream of profanity during their trek. At around 11:00 a.m., the couple reached the farm. Aramis noted that "the farmer was cordial, but his enthusiasm, if any, was not showing."

Nevertheless, the farmer offered to let Virginia stay at a modest one-room house he owned by the roadside. It had a stove that didn't work, and no electricity or water, but it was an inconspicuous place for Virginia to conduct her business. The farmer arranged for Virginia to work and take meals at his own house at the far side of the village. Fortunately, spring was in the air and the weather was becoming more pleasant.

Aramis returned to Paris to begin his own work while Virginia broadcast her radio reports to London. Aramis would come back a few more times to visit Virginia, providing her with supplies and passing along messages related to his clandestine activities.

In exchange for her housing, Virginia cooked for the farmer,

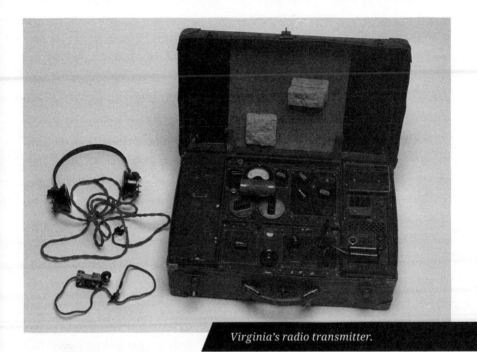

Virginia's radio transmitter.

his elderly mother, and the hired hand. Because there was no working stove in the house, she cooked on the open fire. In her childhood, Virginia never could have dreamed that growing up exposed to farm life in rural Maryland would one day allow her to "live her cover" as an intelligence officer. She later recalled that "my life in the Creuse consisted of taking the cows to pasture, cooking for the farmers on an open fire and doing my W/T work."

Virginia's W/T work would prove invaluable. For example, between July 14 and August 14, 1944, Virginia sent thirty-seven radio messages on behalf of the Maquis to London; some of those messages provided the Allies with valuable information about the movement of German forces.

CHAPTER 17

VIRGINIA TRANSFERS TO THE OSS

While Virginia was in the field, her status changed and she formally transferred from the SOE to the OSS. The change had been a while in coming.

Ever since Virginia completed her first tour of duty in France for the SOE, she was keen on returning, despite the enormous danger to herself because of her notoriety with the Germans. By this time, the SOE and OSS were working closely together. (Indeed, in July 1944, the SOE came under the combined command of British, American, and French authorities and became known as Special Force Headquarters.) At various times since her return to Great Britain, Virginia expressed the desire to transfer to the OSS. But as an OSS official stated, ". . . at the time it was not clear whether she could again be used as an agent in the field and no further action was taken."

Just days before Virginia began her second tour of duty in France as an SOE agent, she met with an OSS official and again made her case for being transferred to the OSS. The official stated:

> I have interviewed the above mentioned lady [Virginia Hall] and I feel confident that the main reason she wishes to transfer from SOE to OSS is for national [presumably patriotic] reason[s] . . . She has been briefed to go in the field as radio operator with an organizer belonging to OSS [Aramis] and she has again expressed a desire to go as an American body. The financial side, that is to say the salary she might earn with OSS has never been discussed and does not seem to worry her in any way. She merely stated that all money she might earn she would like to be sent to her mother, Mrs. E. L. Hall, Boxhorn Farm, Parkton MD. If she is an American body the transfer of funds would be easy whereas if she remains a British body the transfer would be very much more difficult. However the financial improvements she might obtain are not the main purpose for obtaining a transfer.

On April 1, 1944, Virginia officially became "an American body," joining the OSS Western European Section's Special Operations Branch (SO). In her new position, Virginia was to "receive pay and allowances of a 2nd Lieutenant in the US Army, of comparable status, which is in her case $336.00 (single, and not receiving

French Resistance fighters sabotaging the Marseille-Paris railway in August 1944.

parachute pay)." Her entire pay was transferred each month to her mother's bank account in Baltimore, Maryland.

Working with the Resistance was as dangerous as serving with the OSS or the SOE. Acts of sabotage often brought about ruthless reprisals from the Nazis. Virginia and her colleagues were all at great risk. For example, on the same day that Virginia formally became a member of the OSS, the Resistance blew up a railway line at Ascq, France, near the border with Belgium. A train carrying sixty armored vehicles of an SS Panzer Division, along with four hundred German soldiers, was derailed. There was only minor damage and none of the troops were injured.

However, the enraged Nazis went on a brutal rampage, killing the stationmaster and one of his workers. Nazi soldiers then gathered the local men in town to repair the railway, promising that they would soon return to their homes. One of the townsmen recalled what happened next:

We were made to walk for about 15 to 20 minutes until we went through a hole in the fence onto the railway line, beaten with rifle butts as we went . . . There were German soldiers, with a machine gun, on the ground by the track . . . I thought we were going to be put on to the train. As I walked, I saw around 20 to 25 bodies on the ground, and I realized we were going to be shot. We walked a few metres more. The man at the head of our group was a gamekeeper; he was shot at point-blank range by a German. I saw him fall—I was fifth or sixth in line. That was the signal for the Germans by the railway to start shooting. I leaped forward and fell to the ground holding my head in my hands. The shooting carried on. Then everything went quiet. The Germans were walking up and down the path. After a moment, another group of prisoners arrived. They passed barely one metre from my feet and then the shooting began again. After this round of shots, I heard two victims still breathing; a German must have heard them, because there were two shots right next to me. I was kicked twice in the ribs and once in the shoulder, as though to make sure I was dead . . . Eventually a locomotive came and took the train away—it seemed to take forever. I could still hear noises and the sound of Germans on the track. I still didn't dare move. Then a comrade in front of me began to crawl away. I was afraid that the Germans might see him and come and finish us off, but I did the same. Together with a third man we crawled through the field to the Rue Mangin. Then I fled to the other side of the village.

In total, eighty-six men, between fifteen and seventy-five years old, were killed that night.

Despite the danger, Virginia got busy scouting nearby fields suitable for parachute drops and identified "farmers and farm hands willing and eager to help." But it was also clear that Virginia was becoming increasingly exasperated by Aramis:

Aramis came to Maisons twice, but with nothing to report except having found an old family friend whose flat he could use as a safe house. He did not seem to understand using couriers or the advisability of so doing and fiercely resented any suggestions. Aramis was very tired by these trips. In spite of his robust appearance he is not very strong, cannot carry parcels or packages of any weight because he has no strength in his arms, and he was ill for a few days after each strenuous trip that he made.

Virginia established herself within the community of Maisons-sous-Crozant. She worked hard at her farm chores and even took the time to teach neighboring children arithmetic. However, there were a number of security concerns.

Once, Virginia was visited by several OSS agents. While they didn't visit often, there was a chance they could have been followed. On another occasion, the agents failed to keep an appointment, and Virginia feared that something happened to them. Apparently, the true nature of Virginia's mission also became well known in the village, which raised another security concern. Aramis feared that the farmer who owned Virginia's house was talkative. One day, the village postmaster stopped Virginia in the street and "asked her with a twinkle if she received good news these days."

In early May, Aramis returned to Paris, hoping to continue his own covert mission. On his tenth day back in the French capital, he met up with a former comrade with whom he'd served in the French Army in World War I. Through this friend, Aramis was able to connect with a group of Resistance members who rescued Allied airmen and smuggled them back to England through the French underground. Aramis was soon able to establish a *boîte aux lettres*—or mailbox—to communicate with his contacts, as well as a safe house in Paris. Virginia's radio transmissions to London passed along these accomplishments. Additionally, in preparation for the forthcoming D-Day invasion, Virginia transmitted to Aramis orders from London to establish five separate

Virginia outside.

hideaways for radio operators in the geographic triangle of Dijon, Sedan, and Paris. He dutifully set out to accomplish that goal.

Virginia made it a point never to travel alone in France; she always traveled with a French companion. Virginia had become close friends with Madame Rabut, who was introduced to Virginia by Aramis. Madame Rabut served as a courier between the two Americans. Madame Rabut and Virginia traveled to Cosne-Cours-sur-Loire on May 4, where Virginia paid a call on a friend's relative. The man and his wife offered Virginia a place to stay and gave her permission to work in the attic. She was happy to accept this offer. But by this time, Virginia had become increasingly wary of Aramis's talkative tendencies. Accordingly, Virginia requested that Aramis not come to Cosne and not be provided with her new address. Virginia now relied on both Madame Rabut and her son to serve as a liaison between Virginia and Aramis.

A few days later, Virginia was told that several Resistance members had been arrested and detained in the Cherche Midi military prison in Paris. Virginia went to Paris and connected with her Marseille friend who had expertise in getting people out of jail. He was able to contact a sympathetic German guard at the prison, who passed a message to the prisoners.

In response, Virginia found out that the number of prisoners had grown from three to eight, with five more individuals arrested from the same Resistance group. The larger group would be unable to escape in the way Virginia envisioned, and the prisoners wished to stay together. Virginia went to Paris weekly until the beginning of June. At the time of the D-Day invasion, the men were transferred elsewhere.

With the tremendous stress of serving as an undercover agent in a hostile environment, it is important to remain connected to a normal life to the extent that's possible. Family members like to keep in touch with loved ones serving overseas, particularly during wartime. And those serving overseas want to stay connected with their loved ones at home as well. However, it's unusual for undercover intelligence agents in the field to receive letters from their families. This correspondence is usually handled by government officials, who shield the nature, extent, and location of the intelligence agent's work from their family and carefully screen any messages that are passed along. It can be dangerous for agents in the field to have letters from home in their possession as it could compromise their cover and put them at risk.

Virginia's mother, like so many other parents during World War II, only wanted to know how her daughter was doing. For example, on June 2, 1944, just four days before the Allied invasion of Europe, a letter on behalf of a commanding officer in the US military responded to an April 12 letter from Virginia's mother without disclosing the true nature of Virginia's work or the organization for which she was working:

> From a security point of view there is little I am permitted to tell you about your daughter's work. For this I am sorry; it may however be of some consolation to you to know that my own husband knows absolutely nothing of my work; and such is the case of the family of every soldier in our forces. But this I can tell you that your daughter is with the 1st Experimental Detachment of the United States Army; that she is doing an important and time-consuming job which has necessitated a transfer from London, and which will reduce her correspondence to a minimum. Please feel free to write to me, Mrs. Hall. We here are in constant touch with your daughter, and are immediately informed of any change in her status. I shall be happy to communicate whatever news I have of her to you.

At the same time, Virginia, like many agents, seldom wrote home in order to protect her security. For individuals engaged in espionage, operational effectiveness and personal safety were dependent on being discreet about sharing information regarding their work and personal life. Virginia would later remark about seeing the dead bodies of colleagues who lacked that discretion.

Virginia's niece recalled only one letter the family received from Virginia during the war. In it, Virginia described the bodies of French Resistance members being spiked through their necks to iron fence posts, undoubtedly as a warning to anyone else thinking of providing support to the Resistance. Lorna Catling winced at the memory, saying, "Why would anyone write that to their mother?"

CHAPTER 18

SUPPORTING D-DAY AND OPERATIONS IN THE HAUTE-LOIRE

*T*he June 6, 1944, Allied invasion of Europe, also known as D-Day, was the largest military undertaking in world history as approximately 150,000 forces landed or parachuted into Normandy, France. The invasion—including approximately seven thousand vessels, supported by twelve thousand aircraft—brought Allied forces onto French soil for the first time since the evacuation of the British Army from France at the port of Dunkirk in 1940.

Those who survived the war would never forget the invasion, which was a major turning point in the war in Europe. One OSS veteran, speaking of his nighttime D-Day jump into France over

American soldiers storming Normandy Beach on D-Day.

seventy years later, recalled: "It's awful black out there when you look down unless you see a few tracer bullets coming your way."

The foothold that Allied forces gained in France that day opened up a flood of forces and supplies, and quickly became a massive offensive against the retreating German army. The invasion brought about the collapse of the Vichy regime, and most of France would be liberated by October 1944.

The Resistance, in tandem with Allied military forces, had long prepared for D-Day. Virginia's 1944 deployment to France was part of that preparation. The goal of the Resistance was to do everything possible to support the military invasion and bring about the liberation of France. Their main enemy targets were German troop transport, electricity, telecommunications, and railways. The night before the invasion, the BBC broadcast two hundred coded messages in French in the space of fifteen minutes, signaling the groups to activate their offensive operations.

Within twenty-four hours, one thousand acts of sabotage paralyzed France's rail system. Bridges were blown up, trains derailed, and locomotives destroyed, shutting down half the nation's rail system and seriously undermining the German military's ability to send reinforcements to Normandy. The Jedburgh teams were also deployed to coordinate the activities of the Resistance groups with the rapidly advancing Allied forces.

Successful Resistance effort to blow up and derail a train engine.

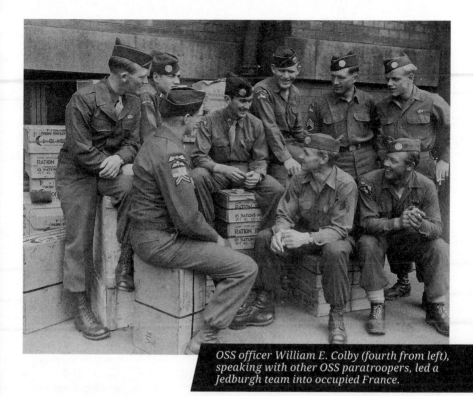

OSS officer William E. Colby (fourth from left), speaking with other OSS paratroopers, led a Jedburgh team into occupied France.

As Virginia and her Resistance colleagues were busy supporting the invasion, the head of the OSS was experiencing his own adventure on D-Day.

General Donovan spent much of World War II at a desk, fighting bureaucratic battles. But he loved to come out to the field and be where the action was. He wasn't going to miss the greatest invasion of the war, particularly when his intelligence officers were doing so much to support the operation.

After landing on the beaches of Normandy, Donovan and his aide, David Bruce, found themselves pinned down by enemy machine-gun fire close to a hedgerow. The two men only had revolvers. Huddled on the ground while bullets whizzed by them, Donovan turned to his aide and said, "You understand of course, David, that neither of us must be captured. We know too much."

"Yes, sir," replied Bruce.

"Have you your pills with you?" Donovan inquired, referring to the poison tablets OSS agents had been issued so that they could commit suicide if they were at risk of being captured and giving up their secrets. Thinking he wouldn't need the tablets, Bruce didn't bring them along. He apologized to his commanding officer.

"Never mind, I have two of them," Donovan whispered, and proceeded to rummage through his pockets. Finally, he realized he had left his pills behind in his London hotel.

Donovan removed his revolver from its holster and peered through a hole in the hedgerow. "I must shoot first," he told his aide.

"Yes, sir," said Bruce. "But can we do much against machine guns with our pistols?"

"Oh, you don't understand," said Donovan. "I mean if we are about to be captured I'll shoot you first. After all, I am your commanding officer." Donovan said he would then shoot himself.

From David Bruce's perspective, the conversation had taken an unfortunate turn. Fortunately, British and American warplanes began bombing the enemy location, and the two men crouched down and ran to safety.

The Normandy invasion finally threw the Germans on the

defensive in France. But there was still much to be done before liberation.

In the weeks surrounding D-Day, Virginia heard little, if anything, from Aramis. To Virginia, it seemed that Aramis wasn't making any progress with his mission. She ultimately concluded, "what the hell," and simply went forward with making the most of things in the area of France where she was working. As a result of her efforts, Virginia had the use of several safe houses for her operators, and she had established a small, discreet group to undertake reception work for Allied servicemen and others seeking to evade the German authorities.

After Aramis acquired his second safe house in Thoury-Ferrotes, he received a letter from Virginia asking for additional information about the hideout. In early July, Virginia sent a letter of thanks and farewell dated June 28, addressed to Madame Rabut, the courier whom Aramis had used to communicate with Virginia. That was the last Aramis was to hear from Virginia.

CHAPTER 19

VIRGINIA GOES HER OWN WAY

*A*t the request of London headquarters, Virginia had been asked to go to the Haute-Loire region in the middle of June 1944. Virginia had told headquarters that there were already 150 men there, but that they had no arms and no direction. They deserved to have a team supporting them. Virginia was directed to fill that leadership void. At the time, she was providing radio support to Antoine, one of her agent colleagues. One of his radio operators had died and the other wasn't capable. Virginia found an agent named Felix as a replacement for Antoine in the first week of July.

Virginia's deputy in the Nièvre, Colonel Vessereau of the gendarmerie, was successful in gaining the confidence of other gendarmes in the Cosne-Cours-sur-Loire district, and recruited approximately one hundred men willing to support the Resistance

A group of French Maquis.

in the Nièvre. They formed a Maquis split into four groups of twenty-five members each.

Around July 9, an agent named Leon, along with Colonel Vessereau, took over the group in the Nièvre. Leon was able to obtain safe houses, couriers, and radio equipment to support the mission, along with one hundred men to organize and train.

During this period, Virginia received no further news from Aramis. When London asked Virginia whether Aramis could be of use to her in the Haute-Loire, Virginia replied in the negative. So Virginia set off on an independent course.

Virginia arrived in the Haute-Loire on July 14, 1944— Bastille Day. She had visited the area the previous month and recalled that "the set up was sound, the men were very good."

At that time, she had provided the men with money for their Maquis group, but they ended up quarreling over the use of it. Five of the men took control of the group, and they were despised by the other Maquis group members. However,

Virginia got along well with these disaffected members, who couldn't return to civilian life and wanted to do something about the German occupiers. Virginia recalled that she "did [her] best for them."

Because no living arrangements had been made for her when she arrived in the Haute-Loire, Virginia stayed with a man named Fayolle and his wife in their house for two days. But she explained to them that aircraft sometimes have detection equipment, and if they detected radio transmissions from their house, it could be bombed. Fayolle found a place for her to stay in a barn at Villonge, close to the Maquis forces. While there, she encountered Lieutenant Bob-Raoul Le Boulicaud, who was an SOE officer and had been living in the mountains for over a year.

Virginia would refer to him as Lieutenant Bob. Virginia found that he "was so solid and so good and his men loved him so much that I took Bob and his particular Maquis of about 30 unto myself." His men were happy to join up with Virginia's forces.

Virginia found herself frequently on the move. She kept busy and was well regarded by her colleagues in the Resistance. The wife of one of Virginia's field operatives spoke admiringly of her courage and devotion to duty, noting that "Miss Hall had never asked for anything but a place to send her radio messages from; that she demanded no personal comforts and slept for days in straw stacks without complaining." Another Resistance official who dealt extensively with Virginia in the summer of 1944 stated: "I noted in Nicolas [Virginia] a great activity, a firm resolution, energy and order and a very great organizing ability. I have only praise for the service she rendered . . ."

After living and working in the Villonge baker's barn for several days, Virginia went to live with Madame Leah Lebrat near Le Chambon-sur-Lignon.

Le Chambon-sur-Lignon (Haute-Loire).

Many of the people in this area were committed to resisting the Germans and the Vichy authorities. The small Protestant community in Le Chambon-sur-Lignon, located in the mountainous Cévennes region, would become famous for helping thousands of Jewish refugees to hide and escape the Nazi genocide.

Madame Lebrat's husband was being held prisoner in Germany, and she had her hands full running her farm and tending to their two children, who were five and nine years old. Nevertheless, her house was always open to help the members of the Maquis, giving them food and refuge. An Alsatian boy, Dede Zurback, lived in the house and helped out with farm chores. He also became a courier as well as an efficient and devoted assistant to Virginia.

Despite the risk to herself and her family, Madame Lebrat took in Virginia without hesitation. Virginia lived with her for two weeks and then moved into an abandoned house belonging to the charitable organization the Salvation Army. The house had three bedrooms—ideal for putting up individuals evading the

Jeffrey Bass's oil painting Les Marguerites Fleuriront ce Soir (The Daisies Will Bloom) *showing Virginia radioing London from an old barn in France.*

German and Vichy forces—with a huge barn that served Virginia well as a workroom. Madame Lebrat supplied Virginia with food, and even sent her a hot meal daily when she was unable to visit the farm. Virginia also acquired bicycles for Dede, another courier, and several of Lieutenant Bob's Maquis "so they could keep in constant touch with me."

Never allowing Cuthbert to keep her from doing her job, Virginia rode her own bicycle as well.

Virginia recalled that "life in the Haute-Loire was different in that I spent my time looking for fields for receptions, spent my day bicycling up and down mountains, scouting fields, visiting various people, doing my W/T work and then spending the nights out waiting, for the most part in vain, for deliveries."

The mountainous, broken terrain of the Haute-Loire made it challenging for Allied pilots to drop supplies with precision, as well as for Resistance reception groups to locate the large containers that sometimes went off course. The metal containers dropped from the sky included weapons, ammunition, batteries, food, clothing, and money. On occasion,

OSS personnel wrapping Bren receivers for packing into parachute containers to be dropped in the field.

Supplies being parachuted to French Resistance members.

Members of the French Resistance searching the sky for Allied airplanes to drop off supplies.

the drops included "stump socks"—medical socks that Virginia needed to protect her leg from her artificial limb. These were a gift from Vera Atkins of SOE headquarters.

In taking the assignment in the Haute-Loire, Virginia made it clear that she would finance and provide weapons to the Maquis, and that they would take orders from her. But she found it difficult to deal with the five men who had previously been in charge of the Maquis and were extremely reluctant to relinquish the power and privileges of leadership. Virginia noted that they "wanted to take everything and give nothing." Virginia felt that it was Dede and Bob's company "who made it possible for me to live and work in [the] Haute Loire."

Any weapons Virginia received went to the Maquis, which she also financed. Her goal was to arm the Maquis members in the mountains and to subdue the thousands of German soldiers then in Le Puy. Despite the fact the Maquis leaders were not particularly cooperative with Virginia, she was happy to support them as long as they were willing to conduct sabotage and guerrilla warfare.

Resistance members study weapon mechanisms dropped by parachute in the Haute-Loire.

As a woman in an environment dominated by men, she didn't hesitate to assert herself. Maquis members at Villonge provided for Virginia's security, but she still was not receiving the men and material she was promised. At the end of July 1944, however, three planeloads of supplies arrived and this made a big difference for Resistance forces. The materials were put to good use, enabling the Maquis to sabotage tunnels and bridges. It also helped to force the Germans out of Le Puy, with five to six hundred of them surrendering.

Virginia didn't take part in sabotage operations. But because of her leadership, the Resistance was able to undertake a number of successful sabotage activities between July 27 and August 12, 1944, which she dutifully cataloged in her activity report when she later returned to London:

- Bridge blown at Montagnac, cutting road Langogne-Le Puy.
- Four cuts made on railroad Langogne-Brassac.
- Freight train derailed in tunnel at Monistrol-d'Allier and fifteen meters of track blown up behind wrecking train and crew after it had gone into tunnel to clear up the wreckage.
- Tunnel at Selignac rendered impassable by blowing up rails.
- Lavoute-sur-Loire [sic]—railway bridge blown.
- Railway bridge wrecked at Chamalieres and locomotives driven into gulf below.
- Telephone lines Brioude-Le Puy rendered useless—lines cut and wires rolled up and telephone posts cut down.

- Between Le Puy and Langeac one *auto mitrailleuse* [armored car] and one lorry [truck] of German soldiers destroyed by bazooka.
- Nineteen *miliciens*—members of the political paramilitary organization created by the Vichy regime to fight against the Resistance—arrested and valuable documents seized.
- German convoy of twelve lorries attacked near St. Paulieu last part of July—FFI [Resistance forces known as the *Forces Francaises de l'interieur,* or French Forces of the Interior] lost twenty killed.
- Five German lorries destroyed around August 12, 1944 near Retournac.
- A convoy from Le Puy was trapped between Chamelix and Pigeyre by bridges blown after five days' struggle to advance. The convoy, which had lost 10 per cent of its effective, surrendered to the FFI of the Loire and Haute Loire at Estiureilles in the Loire. Approximately 500 were taken prisoner—150 killed—FFI losses negligible.
- Le Puy was occupied on August 19, 1944 with 30 Germans killed, 6 wounded—FFI, 5 killed, 4 wounded.

A Jedburgh team from Africa arrived in the middle of August, but they came after the Germans had already been vanquished in the Haute-Loire and Le Puy had been liberated. Nevertheless, the Jeds "did an excellent job" taking on the tasks that Virginia asked of them.

Still, Virginia was plagued with infighting among various Resistance factions. The French member of the Jed team was opposed to the Francs-Tireurs et Partisans (FTP), an armed Resistance group created by leaders of the French Communist Party. Virginia wanted the FTP to be fully integrated as part of the FFI and other Resistance members in order to have a stronger, unified force against the Germans. Virginia met with the FTP Maquis, financed them, and requested that the Jeds take on the task of incorporating them into the larger Resistance effort. Still, the French member of the Jedburgh team said this arrangement was unacceptable.

The Jedburghs had effectively organized the local men at Le Puy and formed three battalions of 1,500 men. However, the

Members of the French Resistance crouch behind a truck during the liberation of Paris.

French Red Cross workers search for identification of Maquis prisoners who were massacred by the Germans as Paris was about to fall to the Allies.

forces still needed extensive training. Virginia financed them and provided whatever weapons she could. When these battalions were formed, Virginia was furious to discover that they were to be deployed to the Belfort Gap in eastern France. She labeled it "a stupid act" to send all those poorly trained men there.

When she raised a complaint, the French military official indignantly asked who she was to be giving orders. Virginia felt that she was not being given the level of support she needed. Exasperated, she noted, "People were sent out ostensibly to work for me and with me but I was not given the necessary authority."

■

Gendarmes, soldiers, and Resistance fighters escorting German prisoners through crowds of jubilant civilians in front of the opera house during the Liberation of Paris.

Victory parade from the Arc de Triomphe down the Champs-Élysées on August 25, 1944.

In another letter to Virginia's mother dated August 23, 1944, the OSS tried to calm her fears about the lack of news regarding Virginia: "I am so sorry to hear that you have been ill, and I fully realize how upsetting Virginia's silence must have been. You must not worry, Mrs. Hall. Virginia is doing a spectacular, man-sized job, and her progress is rapid and sure. You have every reason to be proud of her."

While Virginia was dealing with her organizational headaches, the Allies were surging through France. A major victory for Virginia and her Resistance colleagues came on August 25, 1944, when German forces in Paris surrendered to the Allies.

As directed in his original OSS instructions, Aramis was present for the liberation of Paris. For his work establishing safe hideouts for use as meeting places for intelligence agents and leaders of the Resistance, as well as his subsequent efforts at organizing Resistance groups and providing the location of German strongpoints that assisted French forces in the liberation of Paris, Aramis would later be awarded the Silver Star.

However, Aramis remained puzzled and bitter that Virginia had left him earlier that summer. When he departed Paris for London and summarized his time in France, Aramis wrote that "all in all, I do not think I did as much as I could have done if my radio operator hadn't left me. I do not know if she received formal orders to drop me as she did, but I still doubt that London was willing to leave me without liaison at all. I feel I have done all I could under the circumstances and I wish I could have done more."

CHAPTER 20

RAFAEL AND HEMON FALL FROM THE SKY

*O*n the evening of September 4, 1944, Virginia found herself in a French countryside field. She was contacting a plane with her Eureka radio navigation system and signaling her location so the Jedburgh team members could land on target. The two men who dropped into Virginia's world that night were among the most impressive colleagues she would encounter during the war, and one of the men would become an important part of her life.

OSS officers Second Lieutenant Henry Riley and Second Lieutenant Paul Goillot were waiting to parachute out of their airplane over the Haute-Loire region. As members of the Jedburgh team, the pair were tasked with joining Virginia Hall and the Heckler circuit to use guerrilla warfare and sabotage to harass German forces at every opportunity. Paul and Henry were dressed in civilian clothes the night they parachuted into France.

They both knew that, in addition to the dangers of possible combat, they would be treated as spies and would likely be tortured to death if captured.

Henry Drinker Riley Jr., code name Rafael, was born in Philadelphia in 1916. He was fluent in French and had attended Princeton University. The twenty-seven-year-old had owned and managed a farm in Cuba, exporting fruit to the United States. Henry joined the US Army in August 1943, and on April 19, 1944, he joined his older brother and transferred into the OSS. His specialized skills were military intelligence and weapons demolition. His superiors noted that Henry "is an outstanding troop leader. Extremely reliable, conscientious and with great sense of responsibility. Has the ability to get the utmost efficiency and cooperation from his men. Is a very rugged type."

The other OSS officer waiting to jump into France that night was Paul Gaston Goillot, code name Hemon, who was born in Paris on July 10, 1914. He came to the United States in August 1926. Paul completed the equivalent of grammar school in New York City and was later employed as a knitting machine operator and

Henry Riley code-named Rafael.

by several restaurants in various capacities. Fluent in French, he was fun-loving and a fine athlete. Paul organized dances and sporting events of all kinds, played soccer, and was an avid bicyclist.

Paul enlisted in the US Army in February 1941 and later joined the mountain ski troops stationed at Camp Hale, Colorado. His occupational specialty was as a linguist. In February 1944, Paul was assigned to the OSS as a staff sergeant and developed expertise as a parachutist. He was promoted to second lieutenant in August 1944 and later became a US citizen on December 1, 1944, while serving in London.

The men's parachute jump did not go well. They were more than thirty miles off the planned landing target where Virginia was waiting for them, apparently the result of a communications failure. As soon as they landed, Henry and Paul spent the rest of the night picking up supply packages that had been dropped along with them. By morning, they were only able to locate three of the five packages. For two hours, the men cautiously approached farms that they feared were inhabited by Germans. They ultimately realized that they had landed in friendly terrain and traveled to their rendezvous point in Le Chambon-sur-Lignon.

Henry and Paul reached a bicycle shop, and the proprietor sent for Dede, Virginia's trusted young courier. Dede informed the men that Virginia was on an inspection tour but would be at her home that afternoon. While waiting for Virginia, Dede arranged transportation to the men's drop point to see if they could find the packages they had lost. They were unsuccessful, but they were able to retrieve the three other packages they had hidden the previous night.

The newcomers were introduced to both Lieutenant Bob and Lieutenant Payot, an FTP lieutenant who had joined forces with Lieutenant Bob, and then were taken to Virginia's home. That evening, Henry and Paul passed along messages from London, as well as over two million francs to support resistance operations.

Virginia provided a clear and concise summary of the situation in the Haute-Loire for her two guests; in short: "Everything was over." The German forces had left and were retreating toward their homeland through the Belfort Gap. Virginia was responsible for arming three battalions of resistance forces, and the forces were under the supervision of the Jed team. Reception fields for air dropping of supplies had been selected and reception committees organized. While Henry and Paul realized they had come too late, they resolved to do everything possible to assist Virginia.

The next morning, Henry and Paul met with the Jedburgh team. Henry was surprised to see the Jed team with both an English and a French captain. He had been briefed prior to the mission that the team would only be lower-ranking non-commissioned officers who would be serving under his orders. Now he realized that he and Paul would be outranked, putting them at a disadvantage. While the two men would ultimately get what they wanted out of their counterparts, it only happened after extensive, time-consuming discussions with officers who outranked them.

Initially, Henry and Paul believed that since the Jed team had preceded them by three weeks and had organized the three battalions at Le Puy, there was no point for them to insert themselves into the situation. But the two men ultimately decided to go to Le Puy to assess the situation for themselves.

The next day, Henry and Paul went to Lyon to get gasoline for the three battalions so they could move to Montluçon. The Maquis chief of Lyon informed Henry that there was no gas available for the Americans but noted that the previous day, six thousand liters of gas had been used for the local resistance groups to hold a parade through Lyon. Furious, Henry responded that "it was a dirty way to treat Americans who were working for his country and the war effort." The Maquis chief agreed with Henry and conceded that things were getting out of hand.

Angry and frustrated with their encounter in Lyon, Henry and Paul returned to Le Chambon-sur-Lignon. Virginia had raised the prospect of moving to Alsace to conduct operations, and the two men enthusiastically prepared for that change of plans. The Villonge Maquis selected sixteen men to support this mission, and Henry and Paul immediately set about training them in guerrilla tactics and the use of small arms. The trainees started off with few skills in this area, but because they were highly motivated and "full of fight," they picked up these skills rapidly and became a cohesive fighting unit.

Paul was particularly effective in teaching the men in such short order because of his patience and ability in weapons instruction.

He gave intensive training "to officers and men of the Maquis in the operation and stripping of Light Machine Guns, Bren Guns, bazookas, mortars, English and American rifles and automatic pistols, and also gave the men tactical training in guerrilla warfare and ambushes."

Since August 1, 1944, Virginia had been seeking permission from London to travel to Alsace, in northeastern France, to support operations there, but the request was ultimately refused.

More disappointment came on the evening of September 8, as Virginia and her team waited in vain for an airdrop of supplies. Then again, on the night of September 11, they missed another airdrop and were puzzled why the pilot was unable to successfully connect with the reception committee eagerly awaiting the drop. Henry was able to contact the pilot of one of the planes, who complained that he could not see the signal lights on the field below, despite the fact that Virginia's group had three large automobile headlights mounted on batteries, arranged in the specified position for signaling airdrops.

Finally, Virginia and her team received additional supplies, and it was decided that the group would use a seven-ton truck and three automobiles to form a mobile unit. They mounted a Browning .30-caliber machine gun on top of the truck's cab. They also put Brens, which are light machine guns, on the back of the truck, as well as through the windshield of their reconnaissance vehicle. The group carried additional weapons including .45-caliber revolvers, Springfield rifles, grenades, explosives, and a demolition kit.

Virginia's team then packed up and left to see Isotherme, her contact in Clermont-Ferrand. The remainder of the Maquis were sent into Le Puy, though they would have much preferred to go with Virginia and her team.

The group met with Isotherme at Clermont-Ferrand, and he recommended that instead of going to Montluçon, they should go to Bourg instead. Isotherme provided all the supplies necessary for the trip. On their way to Bourg, they planned to stay overnight in Roanne. The group was told that a band of *miliciens* were situated in the hills outside of Roanne. Learning this, the group formulated a plan in case of attack. But, as Henry remarked, "Much to our regret, we pulled into Roanne without having met any enemy—and in time for dinner."

The following morning, the team proceeded to Bourg and arrived there at lunchtime, and they were directed east to Seventh Army headquarters at Lons-le-Saunier. Virginia, Paul, and Henry were sent to various military officials who first raised the prospect of them conducting ambush operations and other intelligence work in the Vosges Mountains. While this possibility was under consideration, Virginia and her team were told to return in several days.

While these deliberations were going on, Henry quartered the men in an abandoned chateau over fifteen miles from Bourg. After cleaning up the building, the men were put through a rigorous schedule of hikes, calisthenics, compass work, and warfare tactics. Virginia was delighted by their initiative. She remarked, "These two officers are extraordinarily efficient at getting things done—just the sort I might have wished for from the beginning."

To the disappointment of Virginia and her team, a colonel instructed Virginia and her group not to undertake a mission into the Vosges, contending that it was too risky. Henry and Virginia decided that it was a waste of time to stay on without commitment to a new mission. They offered the men a choice: return to the Haute-Loire or enter the First French Army's Ninth Colonial Division.

Seven members joined the First French Army's Ninth Colonial Division in Lons-le-Saunier, and nine went back to their homes, ultimately joining the regular army. Before the group disbanded, Henry collected the small arms from the men returning to the

Haute-Loire. They were, however, allowed to keep their fighting knives and were each provided with a pistol and six bullets for personal protection on their way home. Virginia and her colleagues gave each of them 3,000 francs in order to get themselves reestablished after having lived in the mountains for a year or more. The men who planned to join the Colonial Division were given rifles, pistols, ammunition, fighting knives, and all the other equipment necessary for military life.

On September 21, Henry and Lieutenant Bob took the Resistance members who wished to enter the First French Army's Ninth Colonial Division to Lons-le-Saunier. They provided the Division with "all the arms, munitions and explosives we

In September 1944, a firing squad in Grenoble, France, carries out the death sentence for six young men convicted collaborating with the Vichy government militia.

had with us." Some returned to the Haute-Loire, while Henry, Virginia, and others returned to Paris the next day.

On September 23, 1944, the OSS in London sent a letter to Virginia's mother, noting that "we have had recent word of your daughter Virginia. She continues to be in good health and spirits, and her work is progressing very well. War news is hopeful and encouraging for us all, and it is not unreasonable to suppose that Virginia will soon be returning home."

Henry and Virginia returned to London on September 26, 1944. Back in London, Virginia made particular note of the excellent work of both Henry and Paul, and the difficulty they encountered dealing with their French military counterparts.

Henry and Paul were second lieutenants and were outranked by the French officers. Their requests were not always honored by the more senior French officers. Nevertheless, the two men took over the *corps francs*, or irregular forces, for Virginia and rapidly "whipped them into shape and immediately developed a fine small body of very loyal men."

Virginia was outspoken about the importance of headquarters giving individuals sufficient authority to complete their missions: "It was distinctly unfair to send men into the field in responsible positions without giving them the rank necessary to enable them to work efficiently, for by not doing so they were given great responsibility without sufficient authority."

She was particularly laudatory to headquarters about the men who met her high standards: "Rafael and Hemon have done excellent work for me and if I go out again I want them and no one else to go with me, but if they are to be in uniform I request that their grades be upped, otherwise we shall be heavily handicapped again. This applies whether we go to China—where face is of great importance—or to Austria or Germany where rank is most highly respected."

Virginia summed up her second tour of duty in France as an OSS officer as follows: "In the Cher and the Nièvre, I was again the milkmaid, took the cows to pasture, milked them and the goats and distributed the milk and was able thus to talk with a lot of people in the very normal course of my activities."

In the activity report she filed with OSS for her time in France, Virginia was asked, "Were You Decorated in the Field?" She modestly responded, "No, nor any reason to be." Others would disagree.

CHAPTER 21

HOPING FOR A FINAL MISSION

*A*fter completing her assignment in France and returning to London, Virginia was anxious to take on a new assignment. As the fight against the Nazis was moving closer to the German homeland, new opportunities were becoming available.

In October 1944, Allen Dulles, who was in charge of the OSS office in Bern, Switzerland, received a recommendation to use Virginia Hall for operations in Austria. He was told of her excellent operational track record in France, her extensive contacts, as well as her knowledge of, and experience in, Austria. Dulles was making a strong reputation for himself with his OSS work during World War II, and he would later go on to great fame as the director of Central Intelligence in the 1950s and early 1960s.

Dulles liked to tell fledgling intelligence officers a story

Allen Dulles, who served as the OSS chief of station during the war.

from his early career. When the United States entered World War I against Germany in 1917, he was serving as a low-level diplomat in the US Embassy in Vienna. With the declaration of war, the American Embassy staff was relocated to Bern, Switzerland, arriving early on Easter Sunday morning. As the junior diplomat, young Dulles was asked to sort files and perform other menial tasks, but he had already made a date to play tennis with a young Swiss woman that afternoon.

At midmorning, Dulles was handed the telephone. A Russian émigré politician requested an immediate meeting.

"On Easter Sunday?" asked the incredulous American diplomat. "Yes."

Dulles did not see the urgency but offered to meet on Monday.

"Too late, too late," the Russian protested.

"Sorry," Dulles replied, "but that's the best I can do."

And because Allen Dulles refused to postpone his tennis date, the future director of Central Intelligence missed a meeting with Vladimir Lenin, who went on to lead the Communist revolution in Russia. Dulles often told this story over the years to underscore his belief that intelligence officers should always be open to new people and opportunities.

The recommendation to Dulles about Virginia Hall apparently had an impact, and by early December 1944, the OSS had planned a new mission for both Virginia Hall (code name Diane) and Paul Goillot (code name Hemon) in which they were to be deployed in Austria as part of Operation Crocus. The object of this mission was to contact and organize resistance groups in Austria, and to transmit to London military and political intelligence. The two were to be flown from London to France, entering the northeastern area of Austria.

Virginia's cover story was to pose as an ethnic German of Austrian-Swedish descent. Under this story, she was representing herself as being born in Smyrna, Turkey, moving to France in 1938, and staying with friends on a farm near Dijon until 1943. From there, Virginia was supposed to have come to Paris to "take on a job of secretarial and general office work in a restauran-teur's and black market dealer's office." Under the OSS cover story, Virginia was then to have worked her way to Austria.

Paul's OSS cover story was that he was a Frenchman, born of French parents in Paris, with practically no knowledge of German. Under the story, Paul:

> ... came to Paris in 1940, where he met an old friend of his father's, a restaurateur, a Luxembourger who was start-ing night clubs for German officers in Paris, and who was also dealing in the black market. He is a chef by trade, having learned the business in Paris after his father's death. The restaurateur readily employed him not only for cooking, but to aid in the black market transaction.

In December 1944, OSS headquarters decided to cancel Operation Crocus but noted that both Virginia and Paul were suited for similar operations, particularly in Austria given Virginia's familiarity with the country. The two would have to wait before returning to the field.

In anticipation of a future operation in Austria, Virginia was transferred administratively from the Western European Section of the OSS to the Central European Section, effective December 16, 1944. Soon thereafter, Paul and Virginia were approved to transfer from London to Caserta, Italy, so they would be better placed to support Central European operations.

CHAPTER 22

THE AUSTRIA MISSION

*B*ack in London, René Défourneaux, a Jedburgh member during the war, was trading war experiences with his friend Paul Goillot one day. Défourneaux mentioned how difficult it had been to fill Virginia's shoes after she left France. He asked Paul, "Have you ever heard of this woman?" He knew of her through her code name Diane.

Paul was incredulous. "Do you mean to tell me that you've never met Diane? Well, you're in luck! She's in London now. I'll arrange for us to meet her for lunch tomorrow."

The next day, Défourneaux went to Grosvenor House, the London officers' club, across from Hyde Park, to meet Paul and Virginia. He arrived early, taking a seat in the ornate lobby next to what appeared to be an elderly lady, "wearing an elegant black dress and a stylish black hat with an expansive brim." He assumed she was "a typical upper crust Brit" and paid no further attention to her. Paul walked up to him and said, "Ah, I see you two have already met!"

Surprised and embarrassed, Défourneaux replied, "No."

After introductions and an exchange of pleasantries, Virginia inquired about mutual colleagues. A few minutes later, they moved from the lobby into the dining room. Défourneaux was stunned to notice that Virginia had a prosthetic leg. He wondered how a woman with this disability could have accomplished all that she had behind enemy lines. Because the Germans were well aware of her work with the Resistance, Défourneaux noted that "she had become a master of disguises, something she continued to practice, for reasons not known to me, here in England." He believed that she had adopted a disguise specifically to make herself look much older than she actually was.

During the meal, Défourneaux and Paul fell into a discussion about the Silver Star military decoration. In response, Virginia "entered into a half-hour-long discourse on America and patriotism and how we had not performed our mission for a medal, fame or other recognition, but for our country." Défourneaux would cross paths with Virginia several more times over the years, and he remembered her as "one of the most courageous, memorable people I have ever known."

But true to her character, Virginia was not interested in recognition. Despite the fact that she had already served two dangerous tours as a spy in wartime France, now, in early 1945, she was still anxious to get back in the fight against the Germans.

At the start of 1945, the tides of war were changing. France had been invaded by the Allies, and the Germans were in retreat, forced to protect their homeland. The OSS continued to press for operations against the occupation forces in Austria. Operation Crocus, the defunct OSS operation to place Virginia and Paul into Austria, had evolved, and the two had now become the Fairmont Team.

By February, plans were in development for Virginia and Paul to be deployed into Austria. Arrangements were being made to provide them with finances, not only to cover their own expenses, but to subsidize their organization and operations.

Because of the strong progress of Allied forces against the Germans, OSS headquarters did not want to attempt a large-scale arming of the Austrian Resistance. Headquarters believed that a relatively small-scale effort, supporting the larger military effort, would be most effective. The goal was to deploy teams of five to ten men preparing to attack priority targets such as railroads, communications, and aircraft on the ground. Once sufficient preparations were made for the planned operations, they would await a specific message on a BBC radio broadcast to execute the particular operation.

Also to be deployed as part of this operation were guerrilla bands of approximately twenty-five to fifty individuals, based in mountain areas, to harass enemy convoys and disrupt enemy communications. Their efforts had to be compatible with the "two basic principles of guerrilla warfare: Stay mobile (hit and run), and never accept a pitched battle with regular troops."

Virginia was told to warn her guerrilla forces against taking on more ambitious tasks, such as liberating a village, as it would impose serious logistical burdens, reduce the group's mobility, and put civilians at risk of Nazi retaliation. Because the Nazis were focused on breaking up the Austrian underground, headquarters admonished Virginia that in recruiting her forces, "you must concentrate on quality of personnel rather than on quantity, so as to be quite sure that each weapon and each pound of explosive will be in the hands of a man who will kill Nazis, obey orders, and keep his mouth shut."

Virginia was to supervise acts of sabotage that would finish the work of Allied aerial bombardment, attacking discreet targets such as a switching station in a train yard, rather than the train yard itself, which could be destroyed easily by bombers. The quality of the targets was also far more important than the quantity of targets. Headquarters requested that Virginia and her team make the following targets a priority, which they should attack at their discretion: (1) the German Air Force (e.g., jet propelled fighters, repair shops, factories, and fuel dumps); (2) fuel and oil targets; and (3) enemy communications.

Additionally, Virginia and her team were to prepare their own target list based on information they collected and developed, inform headquarters about their readiness to attack the targets, and then be able to execute the sabotage when they heard a specific message on a BBC radio broadcast.

Virginia was to be deployed to Switzerland by land. She would ultimately be going on to serve in the field in the Innsbruck,

Austria, area as both the head of her team and the radio operator. One of her team members, with contacts in the Austrian Resistance, would have been infiltrated before her.

Paul Goillot, who would be serving as the demolition and sabotage instructor and contact with local French Resistance members, would be parachuted into the area later. It was understood, however, that Virginia was to be a free agent, operating as the representative of the OSS, and not under the control of any other Resistance organization. In a discussion about the logistical challenges of getting Virginia into Austria, an OSS official dismissed any concerns about Virginia's mobility issues: "Diana crossed Pyrénées at 10,000 ft. [and] seems unafraid of walking."

Once Virginia and her team reached the Innsbruck region, she was to establish contact "with friendly elements existing among the local population and among foreign deported laborers." She was also to collect and report on military intelligence in the area, in particular, information on Nazi government and military facilities; any Nazi plans for continuing their political and military activities after the anticipated Allied occupation; the organization of sabotage and guerrilla teams; and organizing parachute supply operations to support those efforts.

Under the code name Anna Müller, Virginia's cover story was that she was a German subject who was born in Turkey. She came to France in 1938 and worked in Paris. In 1944, Virginia crossed the French border, through Luxembourg, into Germany, where she went to work in a firm in Stuttgart. According to the cover story, she was to have transferred from Stuttgart to Austria, where she would have gone to work for the German security service.

On April 28, Virginia and Paul were in Caserta, Italy, where they had been having preliminary meetings with Austrians to select personnel and equipment they'd need for their planned mission in Austria. They were expected to leave in approximately one week.

However, just three days later, OSS headquarters decided that it was pointless to risk the lives of Virginia, Paul, and their team because of the rapid military developments that were bringing the war to a close. On May 1, 1945, Virginia was sent a cable from OSS headquarters stating that with the Seventh Army only three miles from where she was supposed to conduct operations, her operation was canceled.

As the war in Europe was winding down, Allied support to the French Resistance was becoming publicly known, raising concern about the security of the operators still in the field. For example, the April 1945 edition of the popular American publication *Reader's Digest* contained an article describing American and British support to the French Resistance. It even included a possible reference to Virginia when it stated: "The wireless telegraphy operators, one of whom was an American girl, are the unsung heroes of French resistance."

On May 8, 1945, the Allies formally accepted Nazi Germany's unconditional surrender of its armed forces. Nazi dictator Adolf Hitler had committed suicide on April 30, 1945, as Allied forces rolled over what was left of Germany's forces. This was known as Victory in Europe Day, or simply V-E Day— a day of great celebration in Europe, the United States, and throughout the world. Richard Helms, one of Virginia's OSS colleagues, was in Europe and had somehow acquired a sheet of personal stationery from Adolf Hitler's

Official OSS photo of Richard Helms.

Bavarian mountaintop house, embossed in gold with the Nazi swastika symbol and the dictator's name.

Helms took the opportunity on this momentous day to use a sheet of that stationery to write his three-year-old son in the United States. "Dear Dennis," Helms wrote. "The man who might have written on this card once controlled Europe—three short years ago when you were born. Today he is dead, his memory despised, his country in ruins." The OSS agent continued, "He had a thirst for power, a low opinion of man as an individual, and a fear of intellectual honesty. He was a force for evil in the world. His passing, his defeat—a boon to mankind. But thousands died that it might be so."

Virginia and Paul, who were now in Geneva, Switzerland, left for France that day, undoubtedly celebrating along with millions.

Dear Dennis,

The man who might have written on this card once controlled Europe — three short years ago when you were born. Today he is dead, his memory despised, his country in ruins. He had a thirst for power, a low opinion of man as an individual, and a fear of intellectual honesty. He was a force for evil in the world. His passing, his defeat — a boon to mankind. But thousands died that it might be so. The price for ridding society of bad is always high. Love, Daddy

Helms's letter to his young son on Hitler's personal stationery.

They were headed for Paris but first would spend several days in Lyon.

Virginia Hall's war was over. Like so many others, she was wondering what she would do now that peace had arrived at last.

CHAPTER 23

A FINAL ACCOUNTING

*V*irginia Hall had survived World War II unscathed, a remarkable achievement given the risks she took as an intelligence agent through two separate tours of wartime France. Many others in the Resistance weren't so fortunate, and that included some of the individuals who worked closely with Virginia.

Soon after Virginia had been forced to flee Lyon, Dr. Jean Rousset was arrested on November 13, 1942. The primary accusation the Germans made against him was that he had worked for Virginia Hall, known at the time as Marie Monin. Dr. Rousset acknowledged that he knew Virginia—it would have been disingenuous to deny it given the number of times she stopped by his office. But he told the Germans that he only knew Virginia as a patient and had no knowledge of any of her other activities. Nevertheless, the Germans placed him in solitary confinement for a year at Fresnes Prison on the outskirts of Paris. Afterward, he was sent to Germany, where he was ultimately placed in the infamous Buchenwald concentration camp.

At Buchenwald, he was permitted to serve as a physician, tending to the general prisoner population, as well as one or two former Resistance colleagues from Lyon. This in turn led him to meet, and provide healthcare to, French, English, American, and Belgian prisoners who had served as agents.

After US forces liberated Buchenwald in April 1945, Dr. Rousset returned to Lyon. He brought along with him over 150 medical "fiches" or microfiches—sheets of film containing small images of documents—of American and British prisoners that he had stolen from Buchenwald's medical files. He passed this material

Prisoners at the gates of Buchenwald concentration camp.

on to US military intelligence. These prisoners, some dressed in civilian clothes, had been apprehended by the Germans while trying to reach Allied lines. The Germans brought the prisoners to Buchenwald, where they stayed for two months and refused to provide anything more than their name, rank, and name of their military unit. On October 19, 1944, the Gestapo took them away from the camp.

Dr. Rousset's medical fiches also contained information on English political prisoners, as well as Belgian, French, English, and Canadian agents who were hanged by the Germans on September 14, 1944.

When Eugene Labourier's wife was arrested in March 1943, Labourier was able to escape into hiding, carrying on his Resistance work the best he could. The Germans stripped his home of virtually all possessions and took the seventeen trucks in his garage. When Madame Labourier returned to France from a German concentration camp in May 1945, the couple was reduced to wearing clothes given to them by friends. As a result of his service to the Resistance, Virginia recommended that he be granted his request to purchase used army trucks and to be provided additional assistance to restore his life.

Madame Andre Michel (also known as Maggy) and Monsieur Moran (known as Eugene) were arrested separately by the Germans in the early winter of 1943. Maggy was taken to Fresnes Prison, where she denied doing anything for the Resistance. She was even confronted in prison by Eugene, who had apparently confessed everything to the Germans. Nevertheless, she adamantly denied even knowing Eugene. Virginia stated that "Maggy however stuck to her guns and a very enraged Gestapo was unable to get more than a denial of any knowledge of Eugene" or of Virginia. As a result, the Germans sent her off to the Ravensbrück concentration camp for women in northern Germany. Maggy returned to Lyon at the end of the war, in poor health and without any resources. Virginia recommended that she be recognized for her work and provided compensation.

Monsieur J. Joulian and his wife were arrested in April 1943. He was taken to Fresnes Prison, and his wife was taken to Montluc Prison in Lyon, where her front teeth were knocked out and her arm broken. She was released after two months when attending physicians stated that she would not live much longer if she stayed in the prison. Monsieur Joulian was moved around several times, finally ending up in Mauthausen concentration camp in Austria, where he was liberated by American forces.

When Virginia saw the couple in June 1945, they were still in pain from their experiences as prisoners. She found Monsieur Joulian almost unrecognizable from his imprisonment: "his shins were laid open by blows of a pickaxe, in an effort to persuade him to talk and his back slashed up by a razor blade." While Joulian still owned his factory at the end of the war, he had no money to begin work, nor had he been given any compensation for his work for the SOE. Virginia strongly advocated that this case be opened and examined and that maximum compensation be provided to Joulian and his wife.

After Virginia had fled Lyon in November 1942, Germaine Guerin continued to supply food and shelter to members of the underground in Lyon who needed it. One day, she was at the safe house in the Rue Boileau where "the Siamese twins" were staying. The doorbell rang at an unusual time of day, and Germaine sensed that something must be wrong. She opened the door to see seven members of the Gestapo standing before her. She stalled long enough to allow the twins to slip out of the flat through a window to safety. Germaine was arrested and taken away, careful not to mention the existence of other safe houses, at least one of which was occupied. She was sent to Fresnes Prison, and ultimately to Ravensbrück concentration camp in Germany.

Germaine Guerin was returned to France on April 5, 1945, as part of a prisoner exchange. Her possessions had all been taken by the Germans, and the wealthy benefactor who subsidized much of her efforts to support the Resistance movement was suffocated in a crowded train car on the way to Germany. Virginia recommended that Germaine be recognized for her work and provided compensation.

One evening in April 1943, while having dinner with Eugenie Catin and a woman named Madame Beson at a safe house in Lyon, the Newton brothers' apartment was stormed by the Gestapo. The brothers were imprisoned and tortured by Klaus Barbie, the ruthless head of the Gestapo in Lyon.

During this same time, a woman who worked as a radio operator for a Resistance circuit was arrested in Lyon and interrogated regularly by Barbie. She would later recall Barbie interrogating a Jewish prisoner in the cell next to her:

The cell door opened, he didn't pronounce the prisoner's name, he said, "So, have you decided to talk? You're a bastard," and he took out his revolver . . . He said, "You dirty Jew" and so on . . . I heard the prisoner say, "Please, don't kill me, I'll tell you everything. I'll tell you everything, don't kill me," and then, at the same time, bang, bang, and it was all over. The next day, I quickly asked the person who brought the soup round, "Next door?" and was told, "We tidied everything up, it's finished." Barbie had killed him, he had shot him. We lived bathed in terror.

Interior of a cell at Fresnes Prison.

This was the sort of ordeal the brothers, and so many others, were forced to endure. But they refused to give up any secrets to Barbie, and the following month they were transferred to the Fresnes Prison, where their interrogation continued. Still refusing to talk, they were sent to the Buchenwald concentration camp, where they were able to escape execution by constantly altering their prisoner identification numbers. When Buchenwald was liberated by the Americans the month before the war ended, Artus and Auguste were two of the four surviving British agents left in the camp.

After being arrested with the twins, Madame Eugenie Catin was sent to Fresnes Prison as well as several other prisons. She ultimately wound up at the Holleischen concentration camp in Czechoslovakia. She stayed there until May 1945, when the camp was liberated by American forces. When Madame Catin's husband learned of her arrest, he escaped to the mountains for a while. He returned to their home to find that the Germans had stripped the apartment of all their possessions. Virginia recommended that Madame Catin be recognized for her work and provided compensation.

After Peter Churchill's first mission to France in early 1942 when he worked with Virginia, Churchill made two additional expeditions later that year to Antibes, on the French Riviera. In training another circuit in sabotage, he worked particularly closely with two SOE agents, a wireless operator and a French-born courier named Odette Sansom. The attempts to create an effective Resistance effort were thwarted by internal squabbling,

Peter Churchill and Odette Sansom.

the German invasion of unoccupied southern France in November 1942, and poor operational security.

In an effort to elude capture by the Nazis, Peter moved the remnants of the circuit to Saint-Jorioz, France. After returning to France for consultation, Peter parachuted back into the area in April 1943, and within hours, he and Odette were betrayed and arrested at their hotel in Saint-Jorioz. The couple was initially held by Italian authorities, and they represented themselves as married, with Peter falsely claiming to be a relative of British prime minister Winston Churchill. It was their hope that this claim would make them less likely to be executed as spies. The ruse appeared to work.

The couple was moved to solitary confinement in Fresnes Prison. In February 1944, Peter was moved to Berlin and then sent to Sachsenhausen concentration camp, where he was held with special prisoners. After ten months in solitary confinement there, he was transferred to concentration camps at Flossenbürg and then Dachau. On May 4, 1945, the prisoners were liberated by American troops, and after giving testimony about his former captors, Peter returned to London. For his wartime achievements, Peter was awarded Great Britain's Distinguished Service Order.

Odette had been brutally tortured and threatened with execution. A number of her fellow SOE women prisoners were executed by the Germans. In July 1944, she was sent to the notorious Ravensbrück, where she was starved and beaten. She would, however, survive to be liberated. Odette became a national hero in Great Britain, and she was the first woman to be awarded the George Cross. After her first husband died, she married Peter Churchill in 1947.

With the end of hostilities in Europe, Virginia and Paul took a trip around France to visit some of their primary Resistance collaborators from the war and to collect equipment they used in their operations. They set out by car from Paris on Monday, June 17, 1945, and drove almost a thousand miles. Virginia and Paul found most of their comrades unharmed and in good health. By the time they returned to Paris late that Friday night, they brought back several sets of communications, which they returned to an OSS supply office the following morning.

CHAPTER 24

THE TRUE STORY OF ABBÉ ALESCH

*O*f the agents Virginia encountered during World War II, Abbé Alesch was perhaps the most interesting. His story is a cautionary tale about the importance of adequately vetting agents to determine their reliability.

Virginia had hastily departed Lyon on November 8, 1942. On November 12, the *abbé* left a message for Dr. Rousset, Virginia's valuable assistant. At 6:00 the following morning, Gestapo agents arrested the doctor. A week later, the *abbé* returned and talked to Eugenie, the doctor's maid. She knew nothing of either the doctor's or Virginia's work with the Resistance. Eugenie informed Alesch that the doctor had been arrested. The *abbé* then inquired about Virginia, referring to her as "the English woman" rather than her code name, Marie Monin. Alesch insisted that he must see Virginia's friend, and Eugenie gave him the name and address of Germaine Guerin.

The *abbé* then paid a visit to Germaine Guerin, introducing himself as a friend and associate of Dr. Rousset. Germaine believed him, but her friend, Monsieur Genet, questioned him at length. The *abbé* had little to say about Virginia, but emphasized his relationship with Dr. Rousset. His knowledge about the doctor ultimately persuaded Genet that the *abbé* was reliable. Germaine introduced the *abbé* to two other of Virginia's colleagues, "the Siamese twins." (Ultimately, the brothers would be betrayed by Abbé Alesch.) Like Virginia, the twins distrusted Alesch. Nevertheless, the *abbé* returned periodically to Lyon. Genet was always cordial and took him to dine at restaurants in the city.

After the war, the concierge of the apartments at the Rue Garibaldi informed Virginia that the *abbé* came to stay there and took Madame Guerin's furs away to "put them in safekeeping in Paris." On the morning of April 27, 1943, the *abbé* left the Rue Garibaldi flat, and two hours later, the Gestapo arrived and informed the concierge that the *abbé* was arrested and had talked. At least that's what they told Madame Guerin. After two days spent searching through the two apartments, a van pulled up and virtually all the contents of the apartments were removed, including Virginia's clothes and the trunk of men's clothing that she had stored there.

Several days after that, Monsieur Genet was arrested and taken to the infamous Hôtel Terminus in Lyon for interrogation. At the hotel, Monsieur Genet was observed to be "tightly manacled, with the skin and flesh of his wrist and arms in tatters, his face beaten up." Genet was crammed into a freight car along with 150 other prisoners and shipped to the Buchenwald concentration camp in Germany. He suffocated to death before arriving at the destination.

Virginia later talked to the proprietor of a restaurant in Lyon, who said that he had observed the *abbé* dining with Monsieur Genet. The restaurateur told Virginia, "it must have been that Abbé who sold him" to the Germans.

At the end of the war, Virginia said that "I do not know whether Abbé Alesch was a double agent, or a Gestapo agent. I did not trust him and carefully kept him from knowing who I was (or I tried to) and certainly I kept him away from my aides and collaborators . . . I think that case should be investigated if possible, and the Abbé either brought to justice if he was a double agent or cleared if innocent."

Ultimately, justice caught up with the Abbé Alesch, and Allied authorities found out more about him.

His full name was Robert Alesch, and he was born in Luxembourg in 1906. He would go on to study theology, and in 1933 was ordained a priest in the Roman Catholic faith. He served as a vicar in Davos, Switzerland, until 1935, when he was asked to leave, as he put it: "due to my friendly relations with women of my parish."

Later in 1935, Abbé Alesch found a position as vicar at La Varenne-St. Hilaire outside Paris. In January 1942, he was approached and recruited by an official with the Abwehr, Germany's military intelligence organization. Without much persuasion, Alesch provided reports on the general attitude of the French toward the Germans, and got paid for his reporting.

At the time of his encounters with Virginia and her group in Lyon, Alesch noted that "in working for Miss Hall and her group I had hoped to gain favor with the English without the knowledge of the Germans so that I might have a cover with the English in case I was ever arrested in the future." From his work with Virginia and her group, which he referred to as "War Office Liaison (W.O.L.) Friends," Alesch was able to pass along information to his German handlers.

French Resistance members being escorted to their execution after a trial before a German military tribunal in Paris, April 1942.

In October 1942, Alesch met Major Karl Schaefer, the assistant chief of the German Abwehr III—counterespionage group—in Paris. He asked the *abbé* if it was true that he was working as a courier for the Lyon group, and Alesch replied that it was. Major Schaefer reminded the *abbé* that because he had accepted German citizenship—in an unsuccessful bid to obtain a clerical position—his courier work for Virginia's group could be considered treasonous and he could be executed. However, Schaefer offered Alesch the opportunity to continue working with the Resistance but under his direction.

From that point on, Abbé Alesch became an enthusiastic, paid agent of the Germans while the French Resistance thought he was working for them—a double agent. He recalled that "Schaefer showed me a list of members of W.O.L.'s Friends group which I confirmed as being members and I also added several names to the list which were not known to Schaefer." His cooperation would lead

Abbé Robert Alesch.

to the arrest and death of a number of Resistance members.

To be a double agent meant to live a double life. While serving as a vicar at St. Hilaire, Alesch would wear his clerical robes but would change into civilian clothes when he was undertaking his espionage activities. After he resigned his clerical position at St. Hilaire in 1943, Alesch worked with his Nazi handler, Kommandant

Schaefer, in arresting approximately twenty-five Resistance members in Lyon.

Up until the time Paris was liberated, Alesch, at Schaefer's direction, was told to put on his clerical garb and go to Fresnes Prison to hear the confession of French Catholics who were incarcerated there. While offering the prisoners the sacrament of penance, Alesch extracted information provided to him in confidence and passed it along to Kommandant Schaefer.

Alesch was fluent in French, English, German, Italian, Spanish, and Russian. After the war the US Counterintelligence Corps (CIC) noted that Alesch "has the facility and intelligence to assume the identity of any of the above-mentioned nationalities." He was generally successful in persuading people for much of his time as a double agent for the Germans that he was in frequent contact with London as a British intelligence agent. The CIC also noted that "another proven charge against Alesch is the fact that he directly caused the death of twenty Resistance members in Normandy."

Several days before Paris was liberated in August 1944, Alesch fled the city for Brussels, where he obtained a position as priest at a refugee center. He remained there until May 1945 when he posed as a British intelligence agent. On May 18, he visited an uncle in Luxembourg who informed Alesch that American authorities were making inquiries about him. He immediately returned to Brussels.

A few minutes after 6:00 p.m. on July 2, 1945, an officer in the US Army's CIC and another officer arrested Abbé Robert Alesch at the entrance to a Belgian military installation near Brussels. The arrest was made based on a tip from a Belgian soldier. The *abbé* was not wearing clerical robes, but a suit, tie, and a gray felt hat. He carried identification claiming that he was Rene Martin, but he conceded that he was, in fact, Robert Alesch, and that he had discarded his clerical robes to evade arrest after he learned that American authorities were looking for him.

Why did he spy for the Germans? Ultimately, he did it for the money, and the Germans successfully appealed to the priest's considerable vanity. As he explained after the war in 1946:

> Having no experience in the espionage domain, I had hoped to free myself after a while and return to my first convictions. But I became aware that I was caught in a spiral beyond my control. Moreover, the Germans flattered me with compliments that were not undeserved. They admired my knowledge of languages, my psychological finesse, and even my innate sense of adventure. As to myself, I felt that this new occupation took advantage of a weak spot in my soul of which I had been previously unaware, and that it ended up pleasing me.

Eventually, Alesch was handed over to the French authorities, and he was tried and sentenced to death by the Cour de Justice de la Seine on May 26, 1948. He was executed by firing squad on January 25, 1949, at the Fort de Montrouge in Paris.

RECOGNITION

*A*s the war ended, people took stock of Virginia Hall's important contributions in France's liberation. She had been recognized by the government of Great Britain for her first tour of duty in France as an SOE agent by being given the prestigious Member of the Order of the British Empire award.

In February 1945, a proposal went forward recommending that Virginia receive the Distinguished Service Cross (DSC), the second highest US Army decoration—after the Medal of Honor—that is awarded for extraordinary heroism.

In a memo dated May 12, 1945, just seven days after Germany surrendered, General Donovan suggested to President Truman that he might wish to make the presentation to Virginia in person:

> Miss Virginia Hall, an American civilian working for this agency in the European Theater of Operations,

has been awarded the Distinguished Service Cross for extraordinary heroism in connection with military operations against the enemy. We understand that Miss Hall is the first civilian woman in this war to receive the Distinguished Service Cross. Despite the fact that she was well known to the Gestapo, Miss Hall voluntarily returned to France in March 1944 to assist in sabotage operations against the Germans. Through her courage and physical endurance, even though she had previously lost a leg in an accident, Miss Hall, with two American officers, succeeded in organizing, arming and training three FFI Battalions which took part in many engagements with the enemy and a number of acts of sabotage, resulting in the demolition of many bridges, the destruction of a number of supply trains, and the disruption of enemy communications. As a result of the demolition of one bridge, a German convoy was ambushed and during a bitter struggle 150 Germans were killed and 500 were captured. In addition Miss Hall provided radio communication between London Headquarters and the Resistance Forces in the Haute Loire Department, transmitting and receiving operational and intelligence information. This was the most dangerous type of work as the enemy, whenever two or more direction finders could be tuned in on a transmitter, were able to locate the transmittal point to within a couple of hundred yards. It was frequently necessary for Miss Hall to change her headquarters in order to avoid detection. Inasmuch as an award of this kind has not been previously made during the present war, you may wish to make the presentation personally. Miss Hall is presently in the European Theater of Operations.

By June 1945, Virginia knew that she would be awarded the Distinguished Service Cross. While she undoubtedly felt honored by the distinction, it was reported to OSS headquarters from the field that Virginia "feels strongly that she should not receive any publicity or any announcement as to her award." Reminding headquarters that Virginia had also requested no publicity for her earlier decoration from the British government,

Virginia's Distinguished Service Cross (left) and (right).

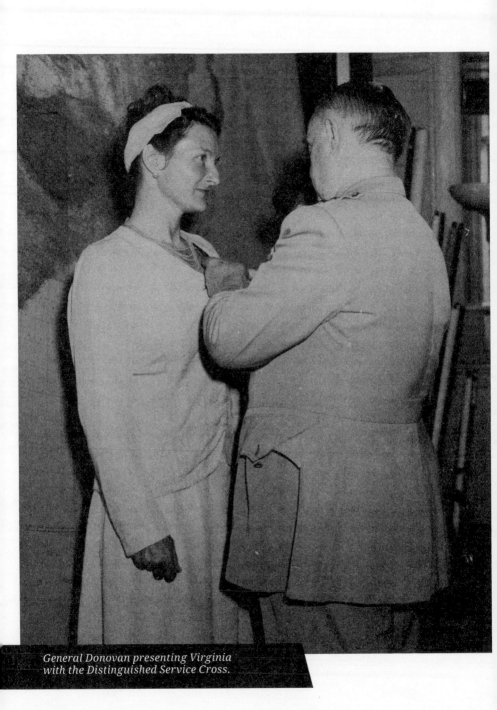

General Donovan presenting Virginia with the Distinguished Service Cross.

she "states she is still operational and most anxious to get busy. Any publicity would preclude her from going on any operation." Virginia was hoping to continue her career in the intelligence field, and she didn't want anything to stand in the way of that.

So, on September 27, 1945, Virginia Hall, accompanied by her mother, received the Distinguished Service Cross from General Donovan in a small private ceremony in his Washington, DC, office. The citation, signed by President Harry S. Truman, read:

Miss Virginia Hall, an American civilian in the employ of the Special Operations Branch, Office of Strategic Services, voluntarily entered and served in enemy occupied France from March to September 1944. Despite the fact that she was well known to the Gestapo because of previous activities, she established and maintained radio communication with London Headquarters, supplying valuable operational and intelligence information, and with the help of a Jedburgh team, she organized, armed and trained three battalions of French Resistance Forces in the Department of the Haute Loire. Working in a region infested with enemy troops and constantly hunted by the Gestapo, with utter disregard for her safety and continually at the risk of capture, torture and death, she directed the Resistance Forces with extraordinary success in acts of sabotage and guerrilla warfare against enemy troops, installations and communications. Miss Hall displayed rare courage, perseverance and ingenuity; her efforts contributed materially to the successful operations of the Resistance Forces in support of the Allied Expeditionary Forces in the liberation of France.

The following day, September 28, 1945, was Virginia's final day working for the Office of Strategic Services. In the letter of resignation she had submitted several days before, Virginia stated: "I am deeply interested in the future of intelligence work and would like to be considered in the event that an intelligence organization is established."

General Donovan and Virginia, with Virginia's mother, after she was awarded the Distinguished Service Cross.

Harry S. Truman had become president upon Franklin Roosevelt's death on April 12, 1945, and saw World War II through to its conclusion. Unlike his predecessor, President Truman was not enamored with either "Wild" Bill Donovan or the OSS. As the United States demobilized and scaled back many of its wartime capabilities, Truman directed that the OSS be closed down over Donovan's strenuous objections. On October 1, 1945, just days after Virginia received the Distinguished Service Cross, the OSS was officially dissolved, with several of its functions being distributed to the State Department and the War Department.

When the OSS was dissolved in 1945, General Donovan arranged for employees to buy a commemorative pin for a dollar.

FOUR

THE CIA

A very hard-working and conscientious person, Miss Hall possesses a high motivation and keen awareness of the importance of our work which are well balanced by a realistic approach based on sound thinking and her own extensive experience in wartime underground operations.

—CIA Personnel Evaluation Report on
Virginia Hall, January 26, 1954

COLD WARRIOR AT THE CIA

*V*irginia was now forty years old and ready to resume life in the United States. She enjoyed intelligence work and had demonstrated an aptitude for it during the war. If at all possible, she wanted to continue to have a career in the intelligence field.

Lorna Catling didn't really get to know her aunt until Lorna was a teenager after World War II. "She was a legend in the family. I knew she was a spy." Virginia was a strong presence, and young Lorna was slightly terrified of her. Virginia was firm in her opinions and knew what she wanted. Her niece observed that she never saw her aunt Virginia get mad, "I just saw her leading in a very strong way."

In December 1946, Virginia went to work in the Strategic Services Unit (SSU), a former component of the OSS. When Virginia joined this organization, it had been moved from the War Department to the Central Intelligence Group (CIG), becoming the foundation of the Office of Special Operations (OSO), the foreign intelligence collection component of the CIG. Because of Virginia's fluency in Italian, she was assigned to the Italian desk, where she collected political and economic intelligence, "with special emphasis on the Communist movement and its leaders." Unsatisfied with the work, Virginia resigned in July 1948.

Virginia's 1946 US passport photo.

Virginia moved to New York City, where in March 1950 she began working for the National Committee for a Free Europe (NCFE), which was located in the Empire State Building. The Committee was secretly acting as the public face of the Central Intelligence Agency (CIA)—in other words, a front organization—associated with Radio Free Europe, which broadcast uncensored news and information to Communist-controlled nations in Europe. Virginia served as the organization's head of the Albanian, Yugoslav, and Baltic desks, handling relations with exiles, translating material, and conducting interviews. She provided guidance and assistance to refugees and groups in those countries in their effort to, in Virginia's words, "keep alive the spirit of freedom and resistance in their native lands in their purpose of bringing about the liberation of all Iron Curtain countries."

Also in 1950, Virginia applied for a job in the new CIA organization. At the end of World War II, the economic, political, and military rivalry between the United States and the Soviet Union and their respective allies created an extended period of tension known as the Cold War. The specter of the atomic bomb raised the stakes in this great power struggle. President Truman came to realize the need for a centralized intelligence organization and signed the National Security Act of 1947, creating the CIA. The Agency became responsible for coordinating the United States' intelligence activities, and evaluating and disseminating intelligence.

Filling out all the applications was "a major operation" for Virginia. While the Agency had undertaken a background investigation of her by the spring of 1950, she stayed with NCFE

Entrance to the original CIA Headquarters at 2430 E Street, N.W., in Washington, DC.

until the end of 1951 when she was sworn in at a CIA office in Washington, DC, on December 3, 1951, as an intelligence operations officer. Virginia joined the Agency on a trial period of one year—at the federal salary level of GS-13 ($8,360 per year). She was forty-five years old.

In 1952, Virginia was one of only six female GS-13-grade intelligence officers in the CIA's clandestine service (and one of only eighteen female GS-13 officers in the Agency). Virginia and her colleagues were the highest-ranking women in the Agency's clandestine service. Virginia would find the CIA to be different from the OSS in a number of respects, particularly when it came to gender equality.

The urgency of World War II had broken down many of the barriers that had prevented women from playing important roles in defending the nation. Women like Virginia were an integral part of the OSS, serving as operational officers, analysts, and support officers. Many of these women came to the new CIA to continue their intelligence careers, but they would find that their salaries and ranks at the Agency did not reflect their previous achievements. For male OSS veterans, it was a different story.

The disparities between the ranks and salaries of male and female CIA employees were so stark that in 1953, director of Central Intelligence Allen Dulles formed an internal review of women's career status at the Agency. The panel included a number of prominent female Agency employees, including several OSS veterans. The so-called "Petticoat Panel" provided a statistical comparison of women's career opportunities at the CIA with opportunities for women in other federal government agencies. It was a bleak picture.

At the time, women made up 39 percent of the Agency's workforce. The panel's report noted that while the median grade for female employees was GS-5, the median grade for men was GS-9. Almost 69 percent of the CIA's male employees served at the GS-7 grade, while only 19 percent of the Agency's female employees were at the GS-7 level or higher. No women ranked above the GS-14 level or held a senior executive position at the CIA, while 10 percent of the male workforce was ranked above GS-14.

This gender inequality would change notably over the decades, but during Virginia's years at the CIA, it was an uphill struggle for women to receive the career opportunities they deserved. Virginia was invariably evaluated by male supervisors who were generally unlikely to have had Virginia's level of operational experience. Indeed, Virginia probably had more operational intelligence experience than many of her male CIA colleagues, including a number of directors of Central Intelligence who ran both the CIA and the entire Intelligence Community.

Virginia began her career at the CIA as a case officer in the Office of Policy Coordination (OPC), the Agency's covert action element, as the head of the paramilitary desk. In this position, she directed and planned paramilitary activities for France, "preparing projects, interviewing and recruiting staff agents, planning training and cover for those agents, and giving support and guidance to the field."

Virginia with two dogs.

Virginia's World War II experiences were excellent preparation for this job. Among her duties was to plan for the possibility of a Soviet invasion of Western Europe. That responsibility included preparing escape and evasion networks of agents, and "stay behind" resistance and sabotage networks, as well as gathering the operational intelligence in support of those agent networks.

As the result of a CIA restructuring in 1952, Virginia became one of the first female operations officers in the new Deputy Directorate of Plans (DDP), where she focused on the Balkans as a member of the Southern Europe Division's paramilitary staff. In her new role, she prepared strategic plans and reports for senior officials, as well as monitored and supported field operations. Acknowledging Virginia's wartime experience, her supervisors stated that she "has an unusually clear understanding of agent operations and problems."

In July 1954, Virginia began a new assignment as an operations officer on the Political and Psychological (PP) staff, reviewing the Western Europe Division's paramilitary and political and psychological activities. She conducted a country-by-country review of the region's plans and operations. Virginia was praised by her managers, "and her experience was deemed her greatest strength."

A CIA official recalled Virginia at the Agency during this time. She was a "gung-ho lady left over from OSS days overseas. Young women in sweater sets and pearls listened raptly to Virginia Hall gas [or "have fun"] with muscular paramilitary officers who would stop by her desk to tell war stories. She was elegant, her dark brown hair coiled on top of her head with a yellow pencil tucked into the bun. She was always jolly when she was around the old boys. She was a presence!"

Virginia was highly regarded for her work at the fledgling intelligence organization. In one of the first personnel reports written about Virginia at the CIA, she was evaluated as follows:

> Generally speaking Miss Hall executes her duties . . . in an excellent manner. Her long experience in the field, including approximately five years as a clandestine agent, assists her materially in carrying out present assignments. She has an unusually clear understanding of agent operations and problems . . . She has consistently

shown her ability to grow with the job and to assume new responsibilities. There is every reason to believe that, given a greater responsibility commensurate with her experiences and talents, she will continue to perform a valuable service for the Agency . . . A very hard-working and conscientious person, Miss Hall possesses a high motivation and keen awareness of the importance of our work which are well balanced by a realistic approach based on sound thinking and her own extensive experience in wartime underground operations. While frank and outspoken in matters relating to her assignment, she is always pleasant, cooperative, and willing to examine objectively differing points of view.

Asked to characterize Virginia's outstanding strengths, her

Formal portrait of Virginia.

manager responded at the end of 1954: "independence, willing to accept responsibility, versatility, experience." And what were her outstanding weaknesses? "[N]one."

Virginia transferred to the CIA's Near East and Africa (NEA) Division in May 1955, continuing her work as a paramilitary officer. Specifically, she was involved in "planning and implementing a major political action project; arranging and preparing for participation in the project as case officer—principal agent." In the first half of 1956, Virginia traveled periodically for her job, presumably to the Near East and Africa regions. She ultimately wrote a report with her conclusions and recommendations about what she had observed in the field.

Virginia's time at NEA was probably the low point of her CIA career. During her tenure in the office, a manager gave Virginia a middling performance rating. The individual who evaluated her stated that she performed most of her duties acceptably but "occasionally reveals some area of weakness." The man rating Virginia conceded that he was "at no time during the rating period in actual supervision of the employee."

Virginia was understandably angry about this performance review and submitted a lengthy rebuttal, asserting that the review was unjustified. She was incredulous that the rater "has written the fitness report on me that he apparently did." Virginia appealed the matter to CIA Inspector General Lyman Kirkpatrick at least three times.

The previous supervisor who had sent Virginia on her temporary duty assignment—and who left to take another position almost immediately thereafter—characterized her performance as "highly competent" and "outstanding." That earlier supervisor blamed NEA for any concerns regarding Virginia, since "without guidance from those offices," he stated, "Hall could not have expected to plan third-country operations based on her survey and should not have been criticized for failing to do so." Virginia's subsequent work ratings were high, and the complaint was apparently an aberration during her tenure at the CIA.

In January 1957, Virginia left NEA to work as an area operations officer at CIA's Western Hemisphere Division. She supervised guidance for Political and Psychological operations in countries in that region, and arranged cover stories and travel for agents. Her supervisors thought highly of her work, noting "her versatility, intelligence, and competence that stood out" and detected "no outstanding weaknesses."

A NEW BEGINNING

*D*espite any frustrations she was experiencing with her work, Virginia found happiness in her personal life. Virginia had maintained a relationship with Paul Gaston Goillot, her Jedburgh colleague. Their relationship had evolved from being wartime colleagues, to friends, to falling in love. After the war, Virginia moved to New York City; Paul lived there as well, working as a chef. It would take almost thirteen years from the time they met in occupied France until the couple got married on April 15, 1957. Virginia Hall, eight years older than her new husband, became Virginia Hall Goillot.

Perhaps part of the long delay in getting married was that Virginia's mother never really cared for Paul. Virginia's niece, Lorna Catling, recalled that in the eyes of Virginia's mother, "he was not good enough for her daughter—period." When Virginia and Paul finally got married, none of Virginia's family attended. Virginia's mother begrudgingly accepted the fact of their

Virginia and Paul with their dogs.

marriage, and until she died in 1965, she was "polite but never very warm to Paul." She saw that Paul made Virginia happy "and nothing was going to change, so she might as well accept it since she loved Dindy too much to cause a break."

After their marriage, Virginia and Paul lived in Chevy Chase, Maryland—a suburb of Washington, DC—then later moved out to a forty-acre farm in Barnesville, Maryland. Paul invested with a partner in a restaurant, with Paul working as the chef. Unfortunately, the business failed and Paul ended up spending his time looking after the farm. The pair loved the outdoor life, enjoying their standard poodles along with the other farm animals. Virginia also liked to make cheese. One of Virginia's favorite hobbies was gardening, and Lorna remembers visiting the farm one spring and seeing an entire hillside covered with daffodils.

Lorna liked Paul tremendously. "He was funny, and a clown, and a tease." Paul and Virginia were extremely close. Virginia was the dominant personality in the relationship, but Paul "didn't mind her bossing him around."

He was shorter than Dindy, but their early married life was fun. They found a great deal of happiness in shared memories. He was good for her. He lightened her life. If she asked him to take a few days off with her and go fishing, he was always ready and obliged.

But Paul's easygoing disposition changed years later after he suffered a stroke.

Virginia continued working at the Agency after getting married. By the early 1960s, Virginia was responsible for all operational planning and activities related to British Guiana and the British West Indies, and her performance ratings by her CIA managers continued to be excellent. Going into 1961, the reviews by Virginia's supervisors made special note of "her knowledge of the region and its personalities, her experience with covert action, and her concise and well-considered dispatches and cables." She was also considered to be especially skilled at identifying flaws in operational proposals made by CIA stations, or offices, in the region.

Virginia (right foreground) at the wedding reception of her niece, Lorna Lee Hall, to Timothy Catling, on June 30, 1956.

In a 1962 evaluation of her work performance, Virginia's manager said that she was "... a superior officer in all respects. She is an experienced person whose work reflects sound judgement, imagination and care for detail. She has been handling one sensitive active operation with regard to British Guiana, in addition to her task responsibilities, in which she consistently demonstrates the above qualities."

In December 1962, eleven years after joining the CIA, Virginia was finally promoted from GS-13 to GS-14—an extraordinarily long time for promotion for an individual of her background and demonstrated ability. At around this time, Virginia received the following performance evaluation:

At present, this employee is the assistant to the undersigned in the conduct of an operation which requires considerable liaison with the British. This employee has an excellent knowledge of the area and the personalities involved. Because of her prior experience, she also has a good understanding of CA [covert action] principles and frequently contributes suggestions ... She prepares well thought out dispatches and cables. She accepts criticism of her work cheerfully and takes steps to correct her errors. She gets along well with her fellow workers and she has given close supervision to the two secretaries who work under her direction ... This employee is cheerful and has a good sense of humor. She is a definite asset in her present position ...

The supervisor who wrote this performance evaluation gave Virginia an overall superior rating. He noted, rather gratuitously, that Virginia lived thirty-five miles outside of Washington, DC, stating that this would make it dif-

An aerial view of the new CIA Head-quarters in Langley, VA, in 1962.

ficult for her to remain after normal working hours or to come into the office at "unusual hours" if necessary, though he conceded that Virginia was willing to do so.

One of Virginia's CIA colleagues observed: "I was distressed at the insensitive treatment accorded Virginia Hall toward the end of her career. No one knew what to do with her, and she was usually at a lonely desk in war plans or the paramilitary offices." He noted that "She was sort of [an] embarrassment to the noncombat CIA types, [by] which I mean bureaucrats. Her experience and abilities were never properly utilized. At the very least she should have been lecturing to trainees at the CIA . . . She was out of the loop, the proverbial round peg, and through no fault of her own. I really ached over her and her low-level status." A number of Virginia's male colleagues at the Agency believed that she had been pushed aside because her extensive experience overshadowed her male counterparts, "who felt threatened by her."

CHAPTER 28

RETIREMENT

*J*n 1966, when Virginia turned sixty years old—the CIA's mandatory retirement age at the time—she left the Agency. She was also suffering from a number of medical issues. Virginia spent her retirement years living with Paul at their home in Barnesville, Maryland.

In retirement, Virginia continued to enjoy gardening; her standard poodles; making cheese; weaving her own cloth on a handloom; solving crossword puzzles; and reading history, spy stories, and travel books from her library.

Virginia's health declined over the years, and she died on July 8, 1982. She was seventy-six years old. *The Baltimore*

Virginia (left) with unknown woman in 1972.

Sun newspaper did not report the cause of her death but noted of her funeral, "With simple services that contrasted to the drama of her World War II career, a Baltimore school girl who became the French underground's 'limping lady' was buried at Druid Ridge Cemetery in Pikesville, Maryland." She was laid to rest

Virginia in a barn with animals.

along with other members of the Hall family. Her husband, Paul, joined her there several years later when he died on April 2, 1987.

In 1943, Virginia had been made an official Member of the Order of the British Empire for her wartime service. But at the time, British officials were unable to locate Virginia to bestow upon her the prestigious Royal Warrant, signed by King George VI and his mother, Queen Mary, who was the Grand Master of the Order. This was rectified sixty-three years later in December 2006 at a ceremony in Washington, DC, where both the British and French governments paid tribute to Virginia Hall.

At the home of the French ambassador to the United States in Washington, DC, the British ambassador presented the Royal Warrant to Lorna Catling on behalf of her aunt. The French ambassador read a letter from French president Jacques Chirac, characterizing Virginia as "a true hero of the French Resistance" and paying tribute to her "indomitable bravery, her exceptional

Virginia's Member of the Order of the British Empire medal (left) and King George's royal signature (right).

selflessness," and calling her a "leader and organizer [who] contributed greatly to the Liberation of France." At the ceremony, a painting was unveiled depicting Virginia radioing London from a barn near Le Chambon-sur-Lignon, in occupied France during World War II, requesting supplies and personnel. The painting is now prominently displayed at CIA Headquarters in Langley, Virginia.

Virginia never sought publicity for her World War II exploits, but as the years passed, historians sought her out to learn more about her extraordinary story. She might have been surprised, and even uncomfortable, to know that her obituary would be published in the *New York Times*. She became an icon, not only for women and people with disabilities, but for those who are fascinated by espionage and stories of heroism during one of the darkest periods in world history.

Like many unsung heroes, Virginia Hall stood up and risked everything to defend liberty. A free and democratic France is part of her enduring legacy.

WORKS
CONSULTED

Binney, Marcus. *The Women Who Lived for Danger: Behind Enemy Lines During World War II*. New York: Perennial, 2004.

Buckmaster, Maurice. *They Fought Alone: The True Story of SOE's Agents in Wartime France*. London: Biteback Publishing Ltd, 2014.

Churchill, Peter. *Duel of Wits: One of the World's Most Famous Secret Agents Tells the Story of His Amazing Adventures in Enemy Territory*. New York: G.P. Putnam's Sons, 1955.

Cobb, Matthew. *The Resistance: The French Fight Against the Nazis*. London: Simon & Schuster UK Ltd, 2009.

Colby, William, and Peter Forbath. *Honorable Men: My Life in the CIA*. New York: Simon and Schuster, 1978.

De Vomécourt, Philippe. *An Army of Amateurs*. Garden City, New York: Doubleday & Company, Inc., 1961.

Dear, Ian. *Sabotage and Subversion: The SOE and OSS at War*. London: Cassell Military Paperbacks, 1996.

Défourneaux, René J., Major US Army (Ret.) *The Winking Fox: Twenty-Two Years in Military Intelligence*. Indianapolis, Indiana: Indiana Creative Arts, 1997.

Escott, Beryl E. *The Heroines of SOE: Britain's Secret Women in France F Section*. Stroud, UK: The History Press, 2014.

Foot, M. R. D. *SOE: An Outline History of the Special Operations Executive, 1940–1946*. With an introduction by David Stafford. London: Pimlico, 1999.

———. *SOE in France: An Account of the Work of the British Special Operations Executive in France 1940–1944*. New York: Frank Cass Publishers, 2004.

Gildea, Robert. *Fighters in the Shadows: A New History of the French Resistance*. Cambridge: Harvard University Press, 2015.

Gordon, Bertram M., ed. *Historical Dictionary of World War II France: The Occupation, Vichy, and the Resistance, 1938–1946*. Westport, Connecticut: Greenwood Press, 1998.

Guéhenno, Jean. *Diary of the Dark Years, 1940–1944: Collaboration, Resistance, and Daily Life in Occupied Paris*. Translated and annotated by David Ball. New York: Oxford University Press, 2014.

Haines, Gerald K. "Virginia Hall Goillot: Career Intelligence Officer." *Prologue: Quarterly Journal of the National Archives* (Winter 1994): 248–260.

Helm, Sarah. *A Life in Secrets: Vera Atkins and the Missing Agents of WWII*. New York: Anchor Books, 2005.

Helms, Richard with William Hood. *A Look Over My Shoulder: A Life in the Central Intelligence Agency*. New York: Random House, 2003.

Irwin, Will, Lt. Col. US Army (Ret.) *The Jedburghs: The Secret History of the Allied Special Forces, France 1944*. New York: PublicAffairs, 2005.

Jacobs, Peter. *Setting France Ablaze: The SOE in France During WWII*. South Yorkshire, England: Pen & Sword Military, 2015.

King, Stella. *'Jacqueline': Pioneer Heroine of the Resistance*. London: Arms and Armour Press, 1989.

Kitson, Simon. *The Hunt for Nazi Spies: Fighting Espionage in Vichy France*. Translated by Catherine Tihanyi. Chicago: The University of Chicago Press, 2008.

Kramer, Rita. *Flames in the Field: The Story of Four SOE Agents in Occupied France*. New York: Penguin Books, 1996.

Le Chêne, Evelyn. *Watch for Me By Moonlight: A British Agent with the French Resistance*. London: Eyre Methuen Ltd, 1973.

Leutze, James, ed. *The London Journal of General Raymond E. Lee: 1940–1941*. With a foreword by Dean Acheson. Boston: Little, Brown and Company, 1971.

McIntosh, Elizabeth P. *Sisterhood of Spies: The Women of the OSS*. New York: Dell Publishing, 1998.

Morgan, Ted. *An Uncertain Hour: The French, the Germans, the Jews, the Klaus Barbie Trial, and the City of Lyon, 1940–1945*. New York: William Morrow and Company, Inc., 1990.

Nouzille, Vincent. *L'espionne: Virginia Hall une Américaine dans la guerre*. France: Fayard, 2007.

O'Donnell, Patrick K. *Operatives, Spies, and Saboteurs: The Unknown Story of the Men and Women of World War II's OSS*. New York: Free Press, 2004.

Pearson, Judith L. *The Wolves at the Door: The True Story of America's Greatest Female Spy*. Guilford, Connecticut: The Lyons Press, 2008.

Powers, Thomas. *The Man Who Kept the Secrets: Richard Helms and the CIA*. New York: Knopf, 1979.

Prados, John. *Safe for Democracy: The Secret Wars of the CIA*. Chicago: Ivan R. Dee, 2006.

Richards, Brook. *Secret Flotillas Volume I: Clandestine Sea Operations to Brittany 1940–44*. With a foreword by M. R. D. Foot. Barnsley, UK: Pen & Sword Books Ltd, 2012.

Rossiter, Margaret L. *Women in the Resistance*. Westport, Connecticut: Praeger, 1986.

Ruby, Marcel. *F Section, SOE: The Buckmaster Networks*. London: Leo Cooper, 1988.

Thomas, Gordon, and Greg Lewis. *Shadow Warriors: Daring Missions of World War II by Women of the OSS and SOE*. Gloucestershire, UK: Amberley Publishing, 2016.

Waller, Douglas. *Disciples: The World War II Missions of the CIA Directors Who Fought for Wild Bill Donovan: Allen Dulles, Richard Helms, William Colby, William Casey*. New York: Simon and Schuster, 2015.

———. *Wild Bill Donovan: The Spymaster Who Created the OSS and Modern American Espionage*. New York: Free Press, 2011.

Weitz, Margaret Collins. *Sisters in the Resistance: How Women Fought to Free France, 1940–1945*. New York: John Wiley & Sons, Inc., 1995.

ENDNOTES

"A remarkable woman . . .": *The Women Who Lived for Danger: Behind Enemy Lines. During World War II*, p. 11

Prologue: Virginia Hall's War

"I felt very much . . .": Letter from Virginia Hall to Margaret Rossiter, February 2, 1978, *Women in the Resistance* papers, University of Michigan Library (Special Collections Library)

"From my point . . .": Denis Rake, Special Operations Executive (SOE) agent, cited by Jacques Chirac, president of the French Republic, December 2006 letter, Lorna Catling collection

As the boat . . . : Activity report by Henry L. Laussucq (Aramis), September 13, 1944, US National Archives and Records Administration (NARA) OSS Archives, College Park, Maryland

Fortunately, the sea was . . . : Ibid.

Part One: A Spy in Training

"I must have liberty . . .": Roland Park Country School yearbook, *Quid Nunc 1924*, p. 12

Chapter 1: The Fighting Blade

Her grandfather, John W. Hall . . . : Associated Press article (untitled), dateline Istanbul, Turkey, January 8, [193-]

He would go on . . . : "Maryland Woman Is Driving Ambulance for French Army: Miss Virginia Hall Joined Allies Last February without Telling Family of Intentions," *The Baltimore Sun*, June 12, 1940, p. 28

John's son, Edwin . . . : *Sisterhood of Spies: The Women of the OSS*, pp. 115–116

Virginia's only sibling . . . : Lorna Catling interview, October 13, 2015

The Halls had . . . : *The Wolves at the Door*, pp. 16–17; Lorna Catling interview

There were hills . . . : *The Wolves at the Door*, p. 16

Virginia once reminded . . . : Lorna Catling interview

"The 'Donna Juanita' . . .": *Quid Nunc 1924*, p. 12

Virginia went to school . . . : Lorna Catling interview

the school's ninth graders . . . : Roland Park Country School alumnae magazine *Connections*, Spring 2007; "The Lady Who Limps," by Nancy Mugele, p. 4

Chapter 2: Student of Europe

But Virginia was impatient . . . : Letter from Virginia Hall to Margaret Rossiter, February 2, 1978, *Women in the Resistance* papers

she spent a year . . . : Virginia Hall's personnel qualification questionnaire, signed by Virginia Hall, December 9, 1952, C01346294, NARA

Virginia also took . . . : CIA biographical profile of Virginia Hall Goillot, date reviewed April 23, 1964, C01346375, NARA

additional courses in French . . . : CIA periodic supplement personal history statement, signed by Virginia H. Goillot on April 2, 1958, C01346345, NARA; *Sisterhood of Spies: The Women of the OSS*, p. 116

made her fluent in French . . . : Virginia Hall's personnel qualification questionnaire, signed by Virginia Hall, December 9, 1952, C01346294, NARA

But she would . . . : Lorna Catling interview

Chapter 3: State Department Years

Virginia once said . . . : Lorna Catling interview

Specifically, Virginia wanted to live abroad . . . : Ibid.

Virginia began her career . . . : Virginia Hall's personnel qualification questionnaire, signed by Virginia Hall, December 9, 1952, C01346294, NARA

Virginia fell in love . . . : Lorna Catling interview

Virginia was involved . . . : Ibid.

Virginia and several friends . . . : Letter from Virginia Hall to Margaret Rossiter, November 17, 1980, *Women in the Resistance* papers

septicemia, or blood poisoning . . . : Letter from Virginia Hall to Margaret Rossiter, February 2, 1978, *Women in the Resistance* papers

An American surgeon . . . : Associated Press article (untitled), dateline Istanbul, Turkey, January 8, [193-]

One night at the hospital . . . : Lorna Catling interview

Virginia never allowed . . . : Ibid.

"a thorough gentlewoman . . .": Letter from F. Egerton Webb to Colonel Edward M. House, January 25, 1938, Franklin D. Roosevelt Presidential Library, Hyde Park, New York

"if anything can be done . . .": Letter from Colonel Edward M. House to President Franklin D. Roosevelt, January 31, 1938, Franklin D. Roosevelt Presidential Library

"Why, Oh, Why . . .": Memo for the secretary of state, February 9, 1938; Ibid

"It seems to me . . .": Ibid.

"I feel deeply . . .": Ibid.

"seriously interfere with . . .": Letter from Cordell Hull to Franklin D. Roosevelt, February 23, 1938; Franklin D. Roosevelt Presidential Library

". . . I have considered . . .": Ibid.

Virginia transferred from Venice in 1938 . . . : Virginia Hall's personnel qualification questionnaire, signed by Virginia Hall, December 9, 1952, C01346294, NARA

the State Department offered . . . : Lorna Catling interview

Virginia left Tallinn . . . : "Miss Virginia Hall," "To: F. From: FB," February 14, 1941, the United Kingdom's National Archives, Kew, Richmond, Surrey. (All material cited from these archives is from Virginia Hall's file, Ref. HS/9/647/4 CG79739. Henceforth, all such sources will be cited as from the UK National Archives.)

Chapter 4: The Gathering Storm

"On May 6, 1940 . . .": "Maryland Woman Is Driving Ambulance for French Army: Miss Virginia Hall Joined Allies Last February without Telling Family of Intentions," *The Baltimore Sun*, June 12, 1940, p. 28

Virginia moved up to . . . : Letter from Virginia Hall to Margaret Rossiter, November 17, 1980, *Women in the Resistance* papers

Virginia sent a letter . . . : "Maryland Woman Is Driving Ambulance for French Army: Miss Virginia Hall Joined Allies Last February without Telling Family of Intentions," *The Baltimore Sun*, June 12, 1940, p. 28

In an interview . . . : Ibid.

On June 16, 1940 . . . : *Historical Dictionary of World War II France*, p. 280

Virginia was in Paris . . . : Letter from Virginia Hall to Margaret Rossiter, November 17, 1980, *Women in the Resistance* papers; "Miss Virginia Hall," "To: F. From: FB," February 14, 1941, UK National Archives

Approximately 1.8 million . . . : *The Resistance*, p. 26

Their living standards declined . . . : Ibid., p. 3

Buildings were covered . . . : Ibid., p. 36

French citizens who supported . . . : Ibid., p. 28

Many young Frenchmen . . . : Ibid., p. 161

The rural guerrilla bands . . . : Ibid, p. 172; *Historical Dictionary of World War II France*, p. 233

"I, General de Gaulle . . .": *The Resistance*, p. 34

Many French citizens listened . . . : Ibid., p. 38

A scholar of the Resistance . . . : Ibid., pp. 50–51

If the uniformed military . . . : Ibid., p. 108

no more than . . . : Ibid., p. 3

the lack of coordination . . . : Ibid., p. 122

Chapter 5: Wartime London: Wearing Life Like a Loose Garment

At a salary of . . . : Virginia Hall's personnel qualification questionnaire, signed by Virginia Hall, December 9, 1952, C01346294, NARA

General Lee, who was . . . : *The London Journal of General Raymond E. Lee: 1940–1941*, p. xiii

Lee was also . . . : Ibid., pp. 22–23

A few days after . . . : Ibid., p. 61

Part Two: A Yank for King and Country
Chapter 6: The New Recruit

They ultimately decided . . . : *The Office of Strategic Services: America's First Intelligence Agency*, by the CIA History Staff, 2007

Prime Minister Winston Churchill announced the creation of . . . : *F Section, SOE: The Buckmaster Networks*, p. 3

"And now set Europe ablaze.": *SOE in France: An Account of the Work of the British Special Operations Executive in France 1940–1944*, p. 13

The component of the SOE . . . : *They Fought Alone*, p. iv

Over 100 of . . . : *SOE in France: An Account of the Work of the British Special Operations Executive in France 1940–1944*, p. 21

The core of . . . : *The Heroines of SOE: Britain's Secret Women in France F Section*, p. 26

The third member . . . : *SOE in France: An Account of the Work of the British Special Operations Executive in France 1940–1944*, p. 95

German listening stations . . . : *The Heroines of SOE: Britain's Secret Women in France F Section*, p. 26

The most sought after . . . : *SOE in France: An Account of the Work of the British Special Operations Executive in France 1940–1944*, p. 42

On Tuesday evening, . . . : "To: F. From: FB," January 15, 1941, CG79739, FB/FR/38, UK National Archives

One month later . . . : "Miss Virginia Hall," "To: F. From: FB," February 14, 1941, UK National Archives

That same day . . . : "Enquiry for Information, Miss Virginia Hall," February 14, 1941, Minute Sheet, S.O.2., UK National Archives

"Will you cause . . .": "To: F. From: FC," April 1, 1941, UK National Archives

The directive concluded . . . : Ibid.

On May 14, 1941 . . . : Official Secrets Acts, 1911 and 1920, UK National Archives

On May 21, 1941 . . . : "Dorothy Schiff Agrees to Sell *Post* to Murdoch, Australian Publisher," by Deirdre Carmody, *New York Times*, November 20, 1976

Backer handed the official . . . : From "MB," May 21, 1941, UK National Archives

That same day . . . : Ibid.

On May 27, 1941 . . . : Ibid.

"I was not trained . . ." Letter from Virginia Hall to Margaret Rossiter, November 17, 1980, *Women in the Resistance* papers

Nor did Virginia receive . . . : Letter from Virginia Hall to Margaret Rossiter, February 2, 1978, *Women in the Resistance* papers

Women were prominent . . . : *The Heroines of SOE: Britain's Secret Women in France F Section*, p. 12 and pp. 34–38

She also stated . . . : Bio form filled out by Virginia Hall, February 2, 1943, UK National Archives

Virginia left for the field . . . : Card signed "Buckmaster" Virginia Hall, UK National Archives

She flew from . . . : *'Jacqueline': Pioneer Heroine of the Resistance*, p. 75

The final leg . . . : Letter from Virginia Hall to Margaret Rossiter, November 17, 1980, *Women in the Resistance* papers

Chapter 7: Virginia's Intelligence Circle

When Virginia arrived in Vichy France . . . : *SOE in France: An Account of the Work of the British Special Operations Executive in France 1940–1944*, p. 154

Once there, Virginia . . . : *SOE in France: An Account of the Work of the British Special Operations Executive in France 1940–1944*, p. 155

Virginia moved to Lyon . . . : Letter from Virginia Hall to Margaret Rossiter, November 17, 1980, *Women in the Resistance* papers

She took on a . . . : *Women in the Resistance*, p. 191

"I was no heroine . . .": Letter from Virginia Hall to Margaret Rossiter, October 2, 1977, *Women in the Resistance* papers

One of Virginia's . . . : Report of Virginia Hall by Maurice Buckmaster, January 15, 1943, UK National Archives

Initially, he served . . . : Ibid.

Virginia informed London . . . : Report to SOE by Marie (Virginia Hall), September 6, 1942, UK National Archives

For some of his medical cases . . . : Subject: Dr. Jean Rousset, 7 Place Antine[?] Poncet, Lyon, To: Chief, SO Branch Forward, June 11, 1945, From: Virginia Hall, NARA

Virginia first met him . . . : Subject: Eugene Labourier, Blvd de la Republique, Le Puy, Haute Loire; report by Virginia Hall, July 10, 1945, NARA

Madame Andre Michel . . . : Subject: Madame Andre Michel, 24 Rue Petite Fusterie, Avignon, From: Virginia Hall, June 11, 1945, NARA

Maggy had a sister . . . : Report of Virginia Hall by Maurice Buckmaster, January 15, 1943, UK National Archives

Another friend and collaborator . . . : Subject: J. Joulian, Fabrique de Lentilles, Rue de La Roderis, Aiguilhe, Le Puy, The Loire, From: Virginia Hall, July 10, 1945, NARA

One of Virginia's . . . : Memo discussing sources in Lyon, "To: F. From: FB," initialed "MB," November 7, 1941, UK National Archives

In a letter . . . : Typed letter from "V.H." to Nic, November 25, 1942, UK National Archives

Germaine Guerin was . . . : Subject: Madame Germaine Guerin, Chez Monsieur

Decley, 29 Jours J. B. Langlet, Reims, To: Chief, SO Branch Forward, From: Virginia Hall, June 1945, NARA

In the summer of 1942 . . . : Ibid.

On August 19, 1942 . . . : *Historical Dictionary of World War II France*, p. 106

Virginia helped arrange . . . : Letter from Virginia Hall to Margaret Rossiter (as transcribed by Lorna Catling), November 17, 1980, *Women in the Resistance* papers; Subject: Madame Germaine Guerin, Chez Monsieur Decley, 29 Jours J. B. Langlet, Reims, To: Chief, SO Branch Forward, From: Virginia Hall, June 1945; NARA

Alfred and Henry Newton were born . . . : *Setting France Ablaze: The SOE in France During WWII*, p. 55

At the end of 1941 . . . : Ibid., p. 56

Arthur was code-named . . . : Ibid., p. 57

Unofficially, London headquarters . . . : Ibid., p. 59

One of the cryptic . . . : Ibid., p. 59

After landing in France . . . : Ibid., p. 62

They got to know . . . : Ibid., p. 63

For her part . . . : Subject: Madame Eugenie Catin, 21 Bix, Rue Xavier Privas, Lyon, To: Chief, SO Branch Forward, From: Virginia Hall, June 11, 1945, NARA

In the early summer . . . : Ibid.

Virginia met with . . . : To: AD/A from F., Regarding Raoul Dautry, October 28, 1941, UK National Archives

She had several . . . : Report of Virginia Hall by Maurice Buckmaster, January 15, 1943, UK National Archives

Chapter 8: Wartime France through a Spy's Eyes

She noted, "The Jews . . ." : Via Western Union to *Post* NYC, Wireless Berne-Lyons, June 22, 1942, Virginia Hall, UK National Archives

She had earlier noted that . . . : Virginia Hall telegram, article to *New York Post*, Little Neck, New York, September 30, 1941, UK National Archives

"the metal collected . . .": Virginia Hall telegram, article to *New York Post*, Little Neck, New York, September 16, 1941, UK National Archives

Virginia also addressed . . . : Cable to *New York Post* at Little Neck, New York, October 1941, by Virginia Hall, UK National Archives the Vichy regime's efforts . . . : Article by Virginia Hall, November 17, [1941?], *New York Post*, UK National Archives

and a woman . . . : Virginia Hall telegram, article to *New York Post*, Little Neck, New York, September 14, 1941, UK National Archives

Virginia even wrote . . . : "La Charmante" by Virginia Hall, September 1942, UK National Archives

As Virginia wrote . . . : Typed letter from "V.H." to Nic, November 25, 1942, UK National Archives

She observed that . . . : Typed memo signed Marie (Virginia Hall), W.O.—055A, April 22, 1942, UK National Archives

"Everybody eats less . . .": "Odd Bits," Lyon, October 1941, Virginia Hall, UK National Archives, Ref. HS 9/647/4 CG79739

"I have been living . . .": Ibid.

But the sisters . . . : Ibid.

Fishing, for example . . . : Ibid.

Virginia noted that . . . : Ibid.

Because of the war . . . : Ibid.

This tended, she . . . : Ibid.

"it's dismal to be . . . ": Ibid.

Virginia argued that . . . : Ibid.

On another occasion . . . : Ibid.

By 9:00 a.m. . . . : Ibid.

Astonished, Virginia said . . . : Ibid.

After the first leg . . . : Ibid.

When the bus . . . : Ibid.

Virginia concluded that . . . : Ibid.

Chapter 9: Taking Care of British Agents

By October 1941 . . . : Summary of Virginia Hall's background, C00024292, NARA

At the time . . . *Historical Dictionary of WWII France*, p. 312

Virginia said, "I can . . .": Typed letter from "V.H." to Nic, November 25, 1942, UK National Archives and she had . . . : Ibid.

and Virginia developed . . . : Letter from Margaret Rossiter to Virginia Hall, September 27, 1980, and Virginia Hall's November 17, 1980, response, *Women in the Resistance* papers

Because of Virginia's . . . : *Sisterhood of Spies: The Women of the OSS*, pp. 116–117

"I'm going shooting . . .": Typed letter from "V.H." to Nic, November 25, 1942, UK National Archives

Several days after . . . : Letter from Virginia Hall to Nic, January 5, 1942, UK National Archives

Virginia went on . . . : Ibid.

Back in December 1941 . . . : *They Fought Alone*, p. 3

Buckmaster had been . . . : *F Section, SOE: The Buckmaster Networks*, pp. 12–13

Buckmaster, along with . . . : *They Fought Alone*, p. 17

Atkins was known . . . : *'Jacqueline': Pioneer Heroine of the Resistance*, p. 77

Lieutenant Churchill was . . . : *Duel of Wits*, p. 21

One evening in January 1942 . . . : Ibid., p. 61

"Mademoiselle is not . . .": Ibid., p. 64

"All I knew . . .": Ibid., p. 66

"Isn't he taking . . .": Ibid., p. 68

As the dinner progressed . . . : Ibid., p. 69

Peter was flattered . . . : Ibid., p. 70

Virginia was impressed . . . : Ibid.

The next day . . . : Ibid., p. 71

Peter gave Charles . . . : Ibid., p. 72

Later, Charles slid . . . : Ibid., p. 77

Then Peter took . . . : Ibid., p. 79

Virginia skillfully maneuvered . . . : Ibid., p. 80

Virginia introduced Peter . . . : Ibid.

The next morning, Peter . . . : Ibid., p. 82

Discouraged and disgusted . . . : Ibid., p. 83

"I suppose they . . .": Ibid.

Now the only thing . . . : Ibid., p. 84

With his mission done . . . : Ibid., pp. 85–86

Another SOE agent . . . : *They Fought Alone*, p. 76

At the outset . . . : Ibid., p. 79

Denis was placed . . . : Ibid., p. 83

From Gibraltar, Denis . . . : Ibid., p. 84

The money had . . . : Ibid., p. 82

Eventually, Denis and . . . : Ibid., p. 96

That first night . . . : Ibid., p. 97

Virginia tapped into . . . : Ibid.

"We should have found . . .": Ibid., p. 97

"I don't much like . . ." : Ibid., p. 98

Clément suggested telling . . . : Ibid., p. 98

"I want a room . . .": Ibid., p. 99

The prostitute explained . . . : Ibid., p. 99

Eventually, the Milice . . . : Ibid., pp. 102–103

For example, two of Virgina's . . . : Memo signed by Marie (Virginia Hall), March 3, 1942, UK National Archives

Virginia complained to London . . . : Ibid.

In a communication . . . : Ibid.

Chapter 10: Abbé Alesch: Friend or Foe?

He told her . . . : Typed report to the SOE by Marie (Virginia Hall), September 6, 1942, UK National Archives

Virginia met the courier . . . : Memo for the officer in charge from Peter Nunez, Special Agent, CIC, Subject: Suspected Gestapo Agents (Alesch, Robert; aliases: de Saint-Martin, Rene; Lambert, Rene; Robert and Georges; Acrin or Acquin, Jean; Frankline, Luxembourger), April 12, 1945, NARA

A British agent . . . : Typed report to the SOE by Marie (Virginia Hall), September 6, 1942, UK National Archives

The *abbé* spoke . . . : From: Virginia Hall, To: Chief, SO Branch, Forward, Subject: Abbé Alesch (Daquin, Aquin, or Jacquin), June 11, 1945, NARA

London responded to . . . : Ibid.

Virginia noted that . . . : Typed report to the SOE by Marie (Virginia Hall), September 6, 1942, UK National Archives

Chapter 11: The River Is Rising: Virginia's Final Days in Lyon

One day in September . . . : From Philomène (Virginia Hall), September 21, 1942, UK National Archives

A contact Virginia . . . : Ibid.

Virginia was ultimately . . . : From Philomène (Virginia Hall), September 30, 1942, UK National Archives

Adding to the . . . : Ibid.

As Virginia noted . . . : Ibid.

Alex and Fabian were . . . : Ibid.

In addition, Pompey . . . : Ibid.

She made the travel . . . : Ibid.

In the first week . . . : Ibid.

One of the British . . . : *The Heroines of SOE: Britain's Secret Women in France F Section*, p. 36

one British agent . . . : *Watch for Me By Moonlight*, p. 68

While her name . . . : From Philomène (Virginia Hall), September 21, 1942, UK National Archives

"The woman who limps . . .": *Sisterhood of Spies: The Women of the OSS*, p. 114

She wrote London . . . : From Philomène (Virginia Hall), September 21, 1942, UK National Archives

But Virginia reported . . . : From Philomène (Virginia Hall), September 30, 1942, UK National Archives

Yet she offered . . . : Ibid.

Virginia was undoubtedly . . . : Ibid. (Virginia was conscientious about providing her headquarters with an accounting of her work and passed along to London a list of her receipts and expenditures, and she was also on the lookout for other operational opportunities. She noted that she could accomplish things in Limoges, over 170 miles from Lyon, if she was either given permission to do it herself, or if she could be sent "a good man for it." She stated, however, that she would be over-extending herself to undertake more work in Limoges, noting that "the only trouble is that I am doing too much as it is and find it hard to swing around the circuit fast enough.")

Chapter 12: Virginia's Escape

On November 5, 1942 . . . : Memo initialed by "MB" with the signature of Virginia Hall, November 5, 1942, passport details were as follows: American passport No. 2019, issued in London on March 31, 1941, renewed in Lyons November 28, 1942, bearing a French visa *aller et retour* (round trip) stamp, valid until February 15, 1943, UK National Archives

Buckmaster requested that . . . : Memo initialed by "MB" with the signature of Virginia Hall, November 5, 1942, UK National Archives

On Saturday, November . . . : From Philomène (Virginia Hall), initialed by "MB," December 4, 1942, Barcelona, Spain, UK National Archives

She immediately began . . . : Ibid.

An agent reported . . . : *Sabotage and Subversion*, p. 145

On Sunday morning . . . : *The Resistance*, p. 148

Virginia was strongly encouraged . . . : From Philomène (Virginia Hall), initialed by "MB," December 4, 1942, Barcelona, Spain, UK National Archives

At 9:00 that evening . . . : "Means of Escape," report by Virginia Hall, January 18, 1943, UK National Archives

As one scholar . . . : *SOE in France: An Account of the Work of the British Special Operations Executive in France 1940–1944*, p. 155

Virginia packed her bag . . . : "Means of Escape," report by Virginia Hall, January 18, 1943, UK National Archives

Virginia left Perpignan . . . : Letter from Virginia Hall to Margaret Rossiter, November 17, 1980, *Women in the Resistance* papers

She stated, "Cuthbert . . .": *Sisterhood of Spies: The Women of the OSS*, p. 118

In the predawn . . . : "Means of Escape," report by Virginia Hall, January 18, 1943, UK National Archives

Virginia was placed . . . : Letter from Virginia Hall to Margaret Rossiter, June 8, 1979, *Women in the Resistance* papers

A younger woman . . . : Letter from Virginia Hall to Margaret Rossiter, November 17, 1980, *Women in the Resistance* papers

Virginia would be . . . : From Philomène (Virginia Hall), initialed by "MB," December 4, 1942, Barcelona, Spain, UK National Archives

And on January . . . : Card signed "Buckmaster" regarding Virginia Hall, [194-], UK National Archives

Chapter 13: On the Sidelines in Spain

She told her SOE colleagues . . . : Report by Virginia Hall (II), Location of W/T sets, January 16, 1943, UK National Archives

In early May 1943 . . . : From: D/F, To: D/R, regarding Miss Virginia Hall, May 5, 1943, UK National Archives

In discussing her . . . : Ibid.

As one official . . . : Ibid.

The bureaucratic transition . . . : Ibid.

She had no . . . : Cipher telegram received from Madrid, July 9, 1943, UK National Archives

"Since August 1941 . . .": Memo, no signature, October 19, 1942, UK National Archives

In a telegram . . . Telegram to Madrid, July 18, 1943, UK National Archives

In early October . . . : "F. from DFV," from Virginia Hall, October 1943, UK National Archives

Maurice Buckmaster responded . . . : Maurice Buckmaster to Virginia Hall, October 6, 1943, UK National Archives

"You are really . . .": Ibid.

He told her . . . : Ibid.

Buckmaster wanted Virginia . . . : Ibid.

Buckmaster conceded that . . . : Ibid.

Soon, Virginia was . . . : To "D/FV," October 7, 1943, UK National Archives

Virginia returned to . . . : Undated profile of Virginia Hall's SOE career, UK National Archives

Part Three: Spying for Uncle Sam
Chapter 14: The OSS: America's Wartime Spy Service

In the years . . . : *The Office of Strategic Services: America's First Intelligence Agency*, by the CIA History Staff, 2007

William J. Donovan was a . . . : Ibid.

At the time . . . : Ibid.

The newly established . . . : *Organizational Development of the Joint Chiefs of Staff, 1942–2013*, Joint History Office, Office of the Chairman of the Joint Chiefs of Staff, April 2013, p. 1

It was decided . . . : *The Office of Strategic Services: America's First Intelligence Agency*, by the CIA History Staff, 2007

By late 1944 . . . : Ibid.

British and American intelligence . . . : Ibid.

The OSS Special Operations Branch . . . : Ibid.

Chapter 15: The Great Adventure: Virginia's Return to France

Philippe de Vomécourt had worked . . . : *An Army of Amateurs*, p. 223

As she later said. . . : Letter from Virginia Hall to Margaret Rossiter, June 8, 1979, *Women in the Resistance* papers

When de Vomécourt met . . . : *An Army of Amateurs*, pp. 223–224

Virginia's OSS companion . . . : Application for employment and personal history statement, June 4, 1943, Henry L. Laussucq, NARA

In August 1943. . . : Activity report by Henry L. Laussucq (Aramis), September 13, 1944, NARA

Aramis's guidance was . . . : Ibid.

Virginia was going . . . : Ibid.

Buckmaster liked to . . . : *SOE in France: An Account of the Work of the British Special Operations Executive in France 1940–1944*, p. 46

The colonel gave Aramis . . . : "Operation Dulverton" and Virginia Hall's transit to France, March 23, 1944, UK National Archives

The next day . . . : Activity report by Henry L. Laussucq (Aramis), September 13, 1944, NARA

The boat was . . . : Undated Virginia Hall note to Margaret Rossiter apparently responding to Rossiter's, May 12, [197-], *Women in the Resistance* papers

Then, as Aramis . . . : Activity report by Henry L. Laussucq (Aramis), September 13, 1944, NARA

Chapter 16: Setting Up Shop

After coming ashore . . . : Activity report by Henry L. Laussucq (Aramis), September 13, 1944, NARA

Next, they were . . . : Ibid.

From the doctor's office . . . : Ibid.

They met up . . . : "The Heckler Mission: Activity Report of Virginia Hall (Diane) the Woman Member of the Team," September 30, 1944, OSS Aid to French Resistance in WWII: RG 226 OSS E 190, Folder 1472, F Section Missions, NARA. (Reports by some OSS personnel covering their participation in F Section operations henceforth to be referenced as "Virginia Hall activity report, September 30, 1944, NARA.")

The following morning . . . : Activity report by Henry L. Laussucq (Aramis), September 13, 1944, NARA

The next day . . . : Ibid.

Nevertheless, the farmer . . . : Virginia Hall activity report, September 30, 1944, NARA

between July 14 . . . : To: Lt Col van der Stricht, From: Lt de Roussy de Sales, narrative on work of Virginia Hall, December 15, 1944, C00024324, NARA

Chapter 17: Virginia Transfers to the OSS

By this time . . . : *F Section, SOE: The Buckmaster Networks*, p. 9

But as an OSS . . . : From: FH/US, To: DR/US, regarding Miss Virginia Hall, March 18, 1944, C00024311, NARA

"I have interviewed . . .": Ibid.

On April 1, 1944 . . . : Western European Section, SO Branch, Subject: Virginia Hall, To Major Robert H. Alcorn from Thomas G. Upton, Captain, F.D., April 3 1944, C00024312, NARA

For example, on the same day . . . : *The Resistance*, pp. 199–200

"We were made to walk . . .": Ibid.

Despite the danger . . . : Virginia Hall activity report, September 30, 1944, NARA

"Aramis came to . . .": Ibid.

Once, Virginia was . . . : Activity report by Henry L. Laussucq (Aramis), September 13, 1944, NARA

In early May . . . : Ibid.

Virginia made it . . . : Virginia Hall activity report, September 30, 1944, NARA

A few days later . . . : Ibid.

"From a security point . . . ": To: Mrs. Hall, From: Charlotte Norris of the 1st Experimental Detachment, June 2, 1944, C00024283, NARA

Virginia would later . . . : *Sisterhood of Spies: The Women of the OSS*, pp. 124–125

Virginia's niece recalled . . . : Ibid., p. 125

Lorna Catling winced . . . : Lorna Catling interview

Chapter 18: Supporting D-Day and Operations in the Haute-Loire

The June 6, 1944 . . . : *The Resistance*, p. 244

One OSS veteran . . . : "He jumped into Normandy, ran spies in Moscow, retired at 90," by Ken Kilanian, November 25, 2015, *Military Times*. (Hugh Montgomery would go on to have a long and distinguished career at the CIA.)

The invasion brought about . . . : *Historical Dictionary of World War II France*, p. 222

The goal of . . . : *The Resistance*, p. 245

Within twenty-four hours . . . : Ibid.

After landing on . . . : *Wild Bill Donovan: The Spymaster Who Created the OSS and Modern American Espionage*, pp. 244–245

In the weeks . . . : Virginia Hall activity report, September 30, 1944, NARA

After Aramis acquired . . . : Activity report by Henry L. Laussucq (Aramis), September 13, 1944, NARA

Chapter 19: Virginia Goes Her Own Way

At the request . . . : Virginia Hall activity report, September 30, 1944, NARA

Virginia's deputy in . . . : Ibid.

Around July 9 . . . : Ibid.

During this period . . . : Ibid.

Virginia arrived in . . . : Ibid.

At that time . . . : Ibid.

Because no living arrangements . . . : Ibid.

The wife of . . . : Subject: Investigation of Report of Virginia Hall + Diane + Nicolas, To: C.O., SO/WE, December 6, 1944, HQ & HQ Detachment Office of Strategic Services European Theater of Operations United States Army SO/WE Section, NARA

After living and . . . : Virginia Hall activity report, September 30, 1944, NARA

The small Protestant . . . : *Historical Dictionary of World War II France*, p. 217

Madame Lebrat's husband . . . : Virginia Hall activity report, September 30, 1944, NARA

Despite the risk . . . : Ibid.

Virginia recalled that . . . : Ibid.

The mountainous, broken terrain . . . : *Women in the Resistance*, p. 195

Virginia noted that . . . : Virginia Hall activity report, September 30, 1944, NARA

Any weapons Virginia . . . : Ibid.

But because of . . . : Ibid.

A Jedburgh team . . . : Ibid.

Still, Virginia was . . . : Ibid.

The Jedburghs had . . . : Ibid.

In another letter . . . : Ibid.

A major victory . . . : *Historical Dictionary of World War II France*, p. 380

As directed in . . . : Silver Star awarded by President Harry S. Truman and presented to Henry L. Laussucq by Major General William J. Donovan, Director of OSS, in Washington, DC, on September 12, 1945, NARA

However, Aramis remained . . . : Activity report by Henry L. Laussucq (Aramis), September 13, 1944, NARA

Chapter 20: Rafael and Hemon Fall from the Sky

On the evening . . . : Virginia Hall activity report, September 30, 1944, NARA

OSS officers, Second Lieutenant . . . : Activity report of 2nd Lieutenant Henry D. Riley, INF. (Rafael), NARA

Henry Drinker Riley Jr. . . . : OSS memo from George F. Ingersoll to Colonel E. G. Connelly, October 23, 1943, NARA

His specialized skills . . . : OSS Confidential Theater Service Record of Henry D. Riley, May 15, 1945, NARA

The other OSS officer . . . : CIA periodic supplement personal history statement, signed by Virginia H. Goillot on April 2, 1958, C01346345, NARA

Paul completed the . . . : OSS background file on Paul Goillot, NARA

The men's parachute . . . : Activity report of 2nd Lieutenant Henry D. Riley, INF. (Rafael), NARA

The newcomers were . . . : Ibid.

Virginia provided . . . : Ibid.

The German forces . . . : Ibid.

Initially, Henry and Paul believed . . . : Ibid.

The next day . . . : Ibid.

Angry and frustrated . . . : OSS background file on Paul Goillot, NARA

Since August 1 . . . : Virginia Hall activity report, September 30, 1944, NARA

More disappointment came . . . : Activity report of 2nd Lieutenant Henry D. Riley, INF. (Rafael), NARA

Finally, Virginia and . . . : Virginia Hall activity report, September 30, 1944, NARA

The group met . . . : Activity report of 2nd Lieutenant Henry D. Riley, INF. (Rafael), NARA

The following morning . . . : Ibid.

While these deliberations . . . : Virginia Hall activity report, September 30, 1944, NARA

To the disappointment . . . : Ibid.

Seven members joined . . . : Activity report of 2nd Lieutenant Henry D. Riley, INF. (Rafael), NARA

On September 21 . . . : Virginia Hall activity report, September 30, 1944, NARA

On September 23, 1944 . . . : To Mrs. Hall from Charlotte Norris, for the Commanding Officer, 1st Experimental Detachment, September 23, 1944, C00024285, NARA

Henry and Virginia . . . : Activity report of 2nd Lieutenant Henry D. Riley, INF. (Rafael), NARA

Henry and Paul were second lieutenants . . . : Virginia Hall activity report, September 30, 1944, NARA

Virginia was outspoken . . . : Ibid.

She was particularly . . . : Ibid.

Virginia summed up . . . : Ibid.

In the activity report . . . : Ibid.

Chapter 21: Hoping for a Final Mission

In October 1944 . . . : Subject: Personnel Survey of Possible Candidates for Staff on Austrian Operations, To: Mr. A. W. Dulles, October 13, 1944, C00024320, NARA

Dulles liked to . . . : *A Look Over My Shoulder: A Life in the Central Intelligence Agency*, pp. 59–60 by early December 1944 . . . : OSS Documents, Operation Crocus, December 1, 1944, RG 226, Folder 1265, Caserta, NARA

Virginia's cover story . . . : OSS Documents, Diane's cover story for Operation Crocus, December 1, 1944, RG 226, Folder 1265, Caserta, NARA

Paul's OSS cover story . . . : OSS Documents, Emmon's cover story for Operation Crocus, December 1, 1944, RG 226, Folder 1265, Caserta, NARA

In December 1944 . . . : From: Bartless and Manning, December 12, 1944, C00024341, NARA

In anticipation of . . . : OSS files, Transfer of Virginia Hall, US Civ, WE/SSO, SO/A/O, December 20, 1944, C00024342, NARA

Soon thereafter, Paul . . . : Subject: Transfer of Personnel, To: Major Eubank, From: Sgt de L'Arbre, December 26, 1944, C00024326, NARA

Chapter 22: The Austria Mission

Back in London . . . : *The Winking Fox: Twenty-Two Years in Military Intelligence*, p. 70

Paul was incredulous . . . : Ibid.

During the meal . . . : Ibid, p. 71

By February, plans were . . . : Virginia Hall financial brief, February 25, 1945, C00024328, NARA

Headquarters believed that . . . : Operations, General Directive, April 7, 1945, RG 226, Folder 1265, Caserta, NARA

Virginia was told . . . : True Name: Virginia Hall, General Directive, April 7, 1945, C00024345, NARA

Virginia was to supervise . . . : Ibid.

Additionally, Virginia and . . . : Ibid.

Virginia was to be deployed . . . : To: Chapin, Caserta, From: Gerry, Bari, Rpt SASAC, Paris, March 25, 1945, C00024268, NARA

Once Virginia and . . . : True Name: Virginia Hall, Final Brief, April 8, 1945, C00024346, NARA

Under the code name . . . : Ibid.

On April 28 . . . : OSS Cable, From Caserta SECRET "Relay to Berne 775 to Gerry from 399," April 28, 1945, C00024245, NARA

However, just three days later . . . : OSS Cable, May 1, 1945, From: Caserta C00024237, NARA

On May 1, 1945 . . . : OSS Cable, May 1, 1945, To: Caserta, "Gerry to 399 Berne for Diana" C00024243, NARA

the April 1945 edition . . . : "Now It Can Be Told: Spark Plugs of France's Secret Army," by Blake Clark, April 1945, *Reader's Digest*, p. 97; OSS Cable, From: Fortullino, May 10, 1945, C00024256, NARA

Richard Helms, one . . . : CIA history website, https://www.cia.gov/news-information/featured-story-archive/2012-featured-story-archive/cia-museum-artifacts-letter-from-helms.html

Helms took the . . . : Ibid.

Virginia and Paul . . . : OSS Cable, OSS outgoing message to Paris from Gerry, June 1, 1945, NARA; OSS Cable, From: Fortullino, May 10, 1945, C00024256, NARA

Chapter 23: A Final Accounting

Soon after Virginia . . . : Subject: Dr. Jean Rousset, 7 Place Antine[?] Poncet, Lyon, To Chief, SO Branch Forward, From: Virginia Hall, June 11, 1945, NARA

After US forces liberated . . . : Ibid.

When Eugene Labourier's wife . . . : Subject: Eugene Labourier, Bvd de la Republique, Le Puy, Haute Loire, report by Virginia Hall, July 10, 1945, NARA

Madame Andre Michel . . . : Subject: Madame Andre Michel, 24 Rue Petite Fusterie, Avignon, From: Virginia Hall, June 11, 1945, NARA

As a result . . . : Ibid.

Monsieur J. Joulian and . . . : Subject: J. Joulian, Fabrique de Lentilles, Rue de La Roderis, Aiguilhe, Le Puy, The Loire, From: Virginia Hall, July 10, 1945, NARA

While Joulian still . . . : Ibid.

After Virginia had fled . . . : Subject: Madame Germaine Guerin, Chez Monsieur Decley, 29 Jours J. B. Langlet, Reims, To: Chief, SO Branch Forward, From: Virginia Hall, June 1945, NARA

One evening in . . . : *Setting France Ablaze: The SOE in France During WWII*, p. 64

"The cell door . . .": *The Resistance*, p. 217

This was the . . . : *Setting France Ablaze: The SOE in France During WWII*, pp. 64–65

When Buchenwald was . . . : Ibid., p. 65

After being arrested . . . : Subject: Madame Eugenie Catin, 21 Bix, Rue Xavier Privas, Lyon, To: Chief, SO Branch Forward, From: Virginia Hall, June 11, 1945, NARA

After Peter Churchill's first . . . : *Setting France Ablaze: The SOE in France During WWII*, pp. 75–77

In an effort . . . : Ibid., pp. 88–89

The couple was initially held . . . : Ibid., pp. 89

The couple was moved . . . : Ibid., pp. 89–90 and 92

Odette had been . . . : Ibid., pp. 90–92

With the end . . . : Memo from Lt. Goillot and V. Hall to Chief, SO Branch Forward, Subject: Trip of Lieutenant Paul G. Goillot and V. Hall to Former Circuits, June 23, 1945, NARA

Chapter 24: The True Story of Abbé Alesch

On November 12 . . . : Subject: Abbé Alesch (Daquin, Aquin, or Jacquin), To: Chief, SO Branch, Forward, From: Virginia Hall, June 11, 1945, NARA

The *abbé* then . . . : *Setting France Ablaze: The SOE in France During WWII*, p. 63

Several days after that . . . : Ibid.

Genet was always cordial . . . : Ibid.

"I do not know . . ." : Ibid.

His full name was . . . : Voluntary Statement of Robert Alesch, signed and subscribed to Peter Nunez, Special Agent, CIC, July 17, 1945, NARA

Later in 1935 . . . : Ibid.

In October 1942 . . . : Ibid.

While serving as . . . : Memo for the officer in charge from Peter Nunez, Special Agent, CIC, Subject: Suspected Gestapo Agents (Alesch, Robert; aliases: de Saint-Martin, Rene; Lambert, Rene; Robert and Georges; Acrin or Acquin, Jean; Franklin, Luxembourger), April 12, 1945, NARA

Alesch was fluent . . . : Ibid.

Several days before . . . : Subject: Robert Alesch, Aliases: Rene de St. Martin; Rene Lammert; Rene Martin; Robert; Georges; Franklin, Luxembourg National Roman Catholic Priests, Former Abwehr Agent for Abwehr III-Paris., Re: Interrogation and Disposition of Subject, signed by Robert Alesch and sworn to by Peter Nunez, Special Agent, CIC, July 18, 1945, NARA

A few minutes . . . : Memo for the officer in charge, by Charles L. Gubellini, Special Agent, CIC, Subject: Robert Alesch (Alias: Rene Daquin; Rene Martin), July 3, 1945, RG 0319, NARA

"Having no experience . . .": *The Hunt for Nazi Spies*, p. 39

Eventually, Alesch was . . . : *Fighters in the Shadows: A New History of the French Resistance*, p. 435

Chapter 25: Recognition

She had been . . . : Memo signed by C. de G., UK National Archives. (In the British archives, there is an undated memo signed by "C. de G."—presumably Charles de Gaulle, leader of the Free French based in London for much of the war. The author notes of Virginia Hall: "Since August 1941, when this lady went into the field on our behalf, she has devoted herself whole-heartedly to our work without regard to the dangerous position in which her activities would place her if they were realized by the Vichy authorities. She has been indefatigable in her constant support and assistance for our agents, combining a high degree of organizing ability with a clear-sighted appreciation of our needs. She has become a vital link between ourselves and various operational groups in the field, and her service for us cannot be too highly praised. In 1944, she inaugurated a new circuit in Central France and by her own efforts in furnishing this circuit with arms and explosives she made it a most powerful factor in the harassing of enemy troops in the area. Miss Hall is most strongly recommended for the award of the Croix de Guerre." Virginia never received this decoration.)

"Miss Virginia Hall . . .": Memo for President Harry S. Truman from William J. Donovan, regarding award of Distinguished Service Cross for Virginia Hall, May 12, 1945, NARA

it was reported . . . : OSS Official Dispatch, SECRET, To: OSS, From: Paris, France, For Action: Director, June 13, 1945, C00024269, NARA

So, on September . . . : Typed letter unsigned by Graham G. Campbell, Lt. Col., Infantry, OSS Citations Officer to the War Department's Adjutant General, notifying that General Donovan presented the Distinguished Service Cross to Virginia Hall (civilian) on this date in Washington, DC, September 27, 1945, NARA

Miss Virginia Hall . . . : Citation for Distinguished Service Cross by Harry S. Truman, OSS file on Virginia Hall, NARA

The following day . . . : Unsigned typed letter from Charles E. Ford to Lt. R. L. Covington, September 28, 1945, NARA. (The letter also notes that Virginia used five days of annual leave during her time with OSS.)

In the letter . . . : Virginia Hall's signed resignation letter from the OSS, to Mr. Whitney H. Shepardson, OSS, Washington, DC, September 24, 1945, NARA

Harry S. Truman had . . . : *Wild Bill Donovan: The Spymaster Who Created the OSS and Modern American Espionage*, p. 4

Truman directed that . . . : *The Office of Strategic Services: America's First Intelligence Agency*, by the CIA History Staff, May 2007

Part Four: The CIA

"A very hard-working . . .": CIA's personnel evaluation report on Virginia Hall (covering February 3, 1952 to December 11, 1953), January 26, 1954, C01346304, NARA

Chapter 26: Cold Warrior at the CIA

"She was a legend . . .": Lorna Catling interview

"I just saw her . . .": Ibid.

In December 1946 . . . : "Virginia Hall's Career in the Central Intelligence Group and CIA," CIA History Staff, unpublished biographical profile, 2015

Because of Virginia's . . . : Ibid.

Unsatisfied with the work . . . : Ibid.

In March 1950 . . . : Ibid.

Filling out all . . . : Ibid.

Virginia joined the Agency . . . : CIA notification of personnel action, December 3, 1951, C01346289, NARA

In 1952, Virginia . . . : "Virginia Hall's Career in the Central Intelligence Group and CIA," CIA History Staff, unpublished biographical profile, 2015

Women like Virginia . . . : *From Typist to Trailblazer: The Evolving View of Women in the CIA's Workforce*, October 30, 2013, Symposium of CIA Information Management Services, CIA Center for Mission Diversity and Inclusion (CMDI), and Smith College, Northampton, Massachusetts, p. 7

At the time . . . : Ibid.

Virginia began her career . . . : "Virginia Hall's Career in the Central Intelligence Group and CIA," CIA History Staff, unpublished biographical profile, 2015

Among her duties . . . : Ibid.

As the result of . . . : Ibid

In July 1954 . . . : Ibid.

A CIA official . . . : *Sisterhood of Spies: The Women of the OSS*, p. 127

"Generally speaking Miss Hall . . .": CIA's personnel evaluation report on Virginia Hall, January 26, 1954 (covering February 3, 1952 to December 11, 1953), C01346304, NARA

Asked to characterize . . . : CIA fitness report on Virginia Hall, December 3, 1954, C01346312, NARA

Virginia transferred to . . . : "Virginia Hall's Career in the Central Intelligence Group and CIA," by CIA History Staff, unpublished biographical profile, 2015

The individual who . . . : CIA fitness report performance of Virginia Hall (covering December 2, 1955 to December 2, 1956), December 28, 1956, C01346327, NARA

Virginia was understandably . . . : Ibid.

Virginia appealed the . . . : "Virginia Hall's Career in the Central Intelligence Group and CIA," by CIA History Staff, unpublished biographical profile, 2015

The previous supervisor . . . : Ibid.

That earlier supervisor . . . : Ibid.

In January 1957 . . . : Ibid.

Chapter 27: A New Beginning

until the couple got married . . . : CIA periodic supplement personal history statement, signed by Virginia H. Goillot on April 2, 1958, C01346345, NARA

Perhaps part of . . . : Lorna Catling email to author, July 17, 2016

After their marriage . . . : Lorna Catling interview

Lorna liked Paul tremendously . . . : Ibid.

"He was shorter . . .": *Sisterhood of Spies: The Women of the OSS*, p .126

But Paul's easygoing . . . Lorna Catling interview

By the early 1960s . . . : CIA fitness report, signed by Virginia H. Goillot on February 23, 1962, C01346360, NARA. (For a brief discussion of Virginia's role in CIA operations at this time, see *Safe for Democracy: The Secret Wars of the CIA*, pp. 10–11)

Going into 1961 . . . : "Virginia Hall's Career in the Central Intelligence Group and CIA," by CIA History Staff, unpublished biographical profile, 2015

She was also . . . : Ibid.

In December 1962 . . . : CIA fitness report (covering January 1, 1963 to March 31, 1963), GS-14, signed June 3, 1963 by Virginia, C01346372, NARA

"At present, this employee . . .": CIA fitness report (covering January 1, 1961 to February 28, 1962), GS-13, signed November 1, 1963 by Virginia, C01346371, NARA

The supervisor who . . . : Ibid.

One of Virginia's . . . : *Sisterhood of Spies: The Women of the OSS*, p. 127

A number of . . . : "Virginia Hall's Career in the Central Intelligence Group and CIA," by CIA History Staff, unpublished biographical profile, 2015

Chapter 28: Retirement

In 1966, when Virginia . . . : Ibid.

Virginia spent her . . . : Notice of change in health benefits enrollment, effective date October 19, 1966, Virginia Hall, Barnesville, MD, C01348524, NARA

In retirement, Virginia . . . : *Sisterhood of Spies: The Women of the OSS*, p. 128

Virginia's health declined . . . : Ibid.

This was rectified . . . : "Allied Countries Honor One of Greatest Spies," *News from France*, Vol. 06.13, December 27, 2006, Ambassade de France aux Etats-Unis

At the home . . . : Ibid.; "British, French Honor US Spy Virginia Hall," December 12, 2006, National Public Radio (www.npr.org)

At the ceremony . . . : *Les Marguerites Fleuriront ce Soir* by Jeffrey W. Bass, Oil on Canvas, 2006, donated by Richard J. Guggenhime, https://www.cia.gov/library /center-for-the-study-of-intelligence/csi-publications/csi-studies/studies/vol52no2 /iac/les-marguerites-fleuriront-ce-soir.html

To know that . . . : "Virginia Goillot Dead; Agent in World War II," *New York Times*, July 14, 1982

PHOTO CREDITS

Photos ©: ix, xvi, xviii, 1, 2 top and bottom, 3 top and bottom, 4: courtesy of Lorna H. Catling; 5 top and bottom: reprinted from the alumnae magazine *Connections* (2007) with permission from Roland Park Country School; 6, 8, 9, 10: courtesy of Lorna H. Catling; 12: courtesy of the CIA Museum; 13, 14 top: courtesy of Lorna H. Catling; 14 bottom: courtesy of the CIA Museum; 15: Franklin D. Roosevelt Presidential Library and Museum; 16: *New York Daily News* Archive/Getty Images; 18: courtesy of the CIA Museum; 19: courtesy of Lorna H. Catling; 21: permission from *The Baltimore Sun*; 22: Heinrich Hoffmann/Getty Images; 23, 24: Keystone-France/Getty Images; 25: Hulton Deutsch/Getty Images; 27: Rue des Archives/The Granger Collection; 30: Franklin D. Roosevelt Presidential Library and Museum; 31: courtesy of Lorna H. Catling; 32: Associated Press/AP Images; 34-35: dikobraziy/Shutterstock; 38: Roger Viollet/Getty Images; 43: courtesy of Lorna H. Catling; 46: courtesy of the International Spy Museum, Washington DC; 50: ullstein bild Dtl./Getty Images; 51: Keystone/Getty Images; 55: courtesy of Lorna H. Catling; 59: Three Lions/Getty Images; 65, 68: Popperfoto/Getty Images; 70: Three Lions/Getty Images; 91: Gabriel Hackett/Getty Images; 94-95: Franklin D. Roosevelt Presidential Library and Museum; 104-105: dikobraziy/Shutterstock; 108, 109, 110: courtesy of the CIA Museum; 111: Colby Family Collection; 113: Roger Viollet/Getty Images; 114: courtesy of the CIA Museum; 115: National Archives and Records Administration; 117, 123: courtesy of the CIA Museum; 126: Roger Viollet/Getty Images; 130: courtesy of Lorna H. Catling; 135: Franklin D. Roosevelt Presidential Library and Museum; 136: Rue des Archives/The Granger Collection; 137: Colby Family Collection; 141: Keystone-France/Getty Images; 143: Roger Viollet Collection/Getty Images; 144: Jeffrey W. Bass; 145: courtesy of the CIA Museum; 146 top: Keystone-France/Getty Images; 146 bottom: Keystone-France/Getty Images; 147: Keystone/Getty Images; 150: Robert Capa/International Center of Photography/Magnum Photos; 151: Franklin D. Roosevelt Presidential Library and Museum; 152 top: Print Collector/Getty Images; 152 bottom: Franklin D. Roosevelt Presidential Library and Museum; 155: National Archives and Records Administration; 159: Alinari Archives/Getty Images; 162-163: Franklin D. Roosevelt Presidential Library and Museum; 166, 175, 176: courtesy of the CIA Museum; 178: Margaret Bourke-White/Getty Images; 182: Gaston Paris/Getty Images; 184: Central Press/Getty Images; 189: Print Collector/Getty Images; 190: National Archives and Records Administration; 195 left and right: courtesy of the CIA Museum; 196, 198: courtesy of Lorna H. Catling; 199: courtesy of the CIA Museum; 200: courtesy of Lorna H. Catling; 204, 205, 208: courtesy of the CIA Museum; 210, 214, 215: courtesy of Lorna H. Catling; 217: courtesy of the CIA Museum; 218: courtesy of Lorna H. Catling; 219: courtesy of the CIA Museum; 220 left: courtesy of the International Spy Museum, Washington DC; 220 right: courtesy of Lorna H. Catling

INDEX

Page numbers in *italics* refer to illustrations.

ACKNOWLEDGMENTS

For seventeen years, I worked on the professional staff of the US Senate Select Committee on Intelligence. My oversight responsibilities frequently took me to the Central Intelligence Agency (CIA) in Langley, Virginia. When time permitted, I visited the CIA Museum—sometimes referred to as "the Best Museum You've Never Seen," since only Intelligence Community staff and official visitors to the CIA Headquarters can visit. Of the many fascinating displays, I was especially intrigued by a gallery dedicated to World War II's Office of Strategic Services (OSS). It was at this exhibit that I first learned about Virginia Hall and became inspired to find out more about her, and ultimately write this book. Jeffrey Bass's painting of Virginia Hall radioing London from a barn in France, *Les Marguerites Fleuriront ce Soir*—prominently displayed at the old CIA Headquarters building—was a further inspiration.

Despite living in a time when being a woman in a field dominated by men and having an artificial leg were viewed as limitations, Virginia Hall was awarded the Distinguished Service Cross—the second highest US Army decoration after the Medal of Honor—for her extraordinary heroism in France during World War II. She was the only woman to receive this distinction for her wartime service.

To a great extent, Virginia Hall has been given short shrift. Most accounts of Virginia's life and service have generally been confined to passing references—or at most a solitary chapter—in books about women intelligence officers during World War II. I'm pleased to have the opportunity to write, and have published, a book exclusively about this exceptional individual who deserves greater public recognition for her courage and achievements.

Biography is the art of compression and interpretation. I hope I've done justice to Virginia Hall and her remarkable life. I appreciate the time and efforts of the individuals and organizations that helped make this book a reality.

I'd particularly like to thank Virginia Hall's niece, Lorna Catling, of Baltimore, Maryland, who was always helpful, gracious, and generous in answering numerous questions about her aunt and sharing her family's archive.

I'm indebted to the scholar Margaret LaFoy Rossiter (1914–1991) for her book, *Women in the Resistance* (1986), which includes a section on Virginia Hall. She donated her research material for her book to the University of Michigan's Special Collections Library in Ann Arbor, Michigan. The collection includes her correspondence with Virginia Hall, which was of great help in obtaining Virginia's perspective on her life and espionage career. I'm grateful to the University of Michigan archivists for their valuable assistance.

The two phases of Virginia's World War II espionage activities were with the United Kingdom's Special Operations Executive (SOE), and the United States' OSS, the CIA's predecessor organization. With the passage of time, these previously classified archives have been opened up to the public, shedding light on World War II's secret war.

I wish to acknowledge the help I received obtaining Virginia's SOE file from Great Britain's National Archives, located in Kew, Richmond, Surrey. I would like to thank the archivists at the National Archives and Records Administration in College Park, Maryland, for their assistance in acquiring files related to the OSS. In particular, I would like to thank Sim Smiley, an independent research specialist, who provided significant research assistance in accessing OSS documents at the National Archives.

I'm grateful to CIA Chief Historian Dr. David Robarge and his staff for their biographical profile of Virginia, which was declassified and obtained under the Freedom of Information Act (FOIA). This document gave me valuable insights into her post–World War II intelligence career at the Agency. I would also like to thank the CIA Museum staff, particularly Museum Director Toni Hiley and Museum Deputy Director for Curatorial Affairs Robert Byer, for their assistance in obtaining photos from the Agency's archive.

I'm also grateful to Amanda Abrell, director of communications at the International Spy Museum in Washington, DC; Nancy Mugele, assistant head of school for external relations for the Roland Park Country School in Baltimore, Maryland; the Franklin D. Roosevelt Presidential Library and Museum in Hyde Park, New York; Nancy Trueheart; and Randy Bookout. Thanks also to Jeffrey Bass and the families of former Directors of Central Intelligence Richard Helms and William Colby.

Special thanks to my editors Jody Corbett and Paige Hazzan, as well as Jael Fogle, Keirsten Geise, Lisa Sandell, Amla Sanghvi, Emily Teresa, Aerin Cisgay, Jeff Paul, Cian O'Day, and Jim McMahon of Scholastic Focus. Thanks also to Susan Cohen, my literary agent at Writers House.

I'm most indebted to my wife, Grace, and our children, Logan and Ella, who have been unfailingly supportive, patient, and understanding in this and every other endeavor I've undertaken. My family has given me great joy, a sense of purpose, and added meaning to my life.

ABOUT
THE AUTHOR

Don Mitchell is a critically acclaimed author of nonfiction for young people, including *The Freedom Summer Murders*, which received multiple starred reviews and was a Kirkus Prize finalist for Young Readers' Literature, an NAACP Image Award nominee for Outstanding Literary Work for Teens, and a Kirkus Best Book of the Year; *Liftoff: A Photobiography of John Glenn*; and *Driven: A Photobiography of Henry Ford*. He has served on the staff of the US Senate Select Committee on Intelligence, as well as on the staff of the National Security Council.